The Leadership Of Muhammad

A HISTORICAL RECONSTRUCTION

The Leadership Of Muhammad

A HISTORICAL RECONSTRUCTION

Joel Hayward

CLARITAS
BOOKS

1 2 3 4 5 6 7 8 9 10

CLARITAS BOOKS

Bernard Street, Swansea, United Kingdom
Milpitas, California, United States

© CLARITAS BOOKS 2021

This book is in copyright. Subject to statutory exception and to the provisions of relevant collective licensing agreements, no reproduction of any part may take place without the written permission of
Claritas Books.

First Published in March 2021

Typeset in Minion Pro 14/11

The Leadership of Muhammad: A Historical Reconstruction
By Joel Hayward

A CIP catalogue record for this book is available from the British Library

ISBN: 978-1-80011-989-5

PROFESSOR JOEL HAYWARD is a New Zealand/British scholar, writer and poet who currently serves as Professor of Strategic Thought at the National Defense College of the United Arab Emirates. He has earned *ijazas* in *'Aqidah* (Islamic theology) and *Sirah* (the Prophet's biography). He has held various academic leadership posts, including Director of the Institute for International and Civil Security at Khalifa University (UAE), Chair of the Department of Humanities and Social Sciences (also at Khalifa University), Head of Air Power Studies at King's College London, and Dean of the Royal Air Force College (both UK). He is the author or editor of fifteen books and monographs and dozens of peer-reviewed articles, mainly in the fields of strategic studies, the ethics of war and conflict, and Islamic and modern western history. His recent books include *Warfare in the Qur'an* (2012), *War is Deceit: An Analysis of a Contentious Hadith on the Morality of Military Deception* (2017), and *Civilian Immunity in Foundational Islamic Strategic Thought: A Historical Enquiry* (2019).

Professor Hayward has given strategic advice to political and military leaders in several countries, has given policy advice to prominent sheikhs, and was tutor to His Royal Highness Prince William of Wales, Duke of Cambridge. In 2011 he was elected as a Fellow of the Royal Society of Arts and in 2012 he was elected as a Fellow of the Royal Historical Society. In 2016 he was named as the "Best Professor of Humanities and Social Sciences" at the Middle East Education Leadership Awards. Professor Hayward is also active in the literary arts and has published three books of fiction and four collections of Islamic poetry.

Disclaimer: The opinions expressed in this book are those of the author and do not reflect the views of the National Defense College or the United Arab Emirates government.

Contents

Map of Seventh Century Arabia	15
Introduction	17
Theocentric Leadership	23
Understanding Authority	31
Consultative Leadership	39
Leading by Example	47
Common Touch	53
Strategic Vision	61
Strategic Communication	71
Military Leadership	85
Maximising Human Potential	99
Diplomatic Leadership	115
Conclusion	131
Postscript: Lessons for Leaders	137
Chronology	143
Glossary	145
Endnotes	147
Bibliography	173
Index	177

For Hasna, my amira
الى حسنا... أميرتي

"It was through Allah's mercy that you [Muhammad] have been able to deal with them so gently. If you had been stern and hard-hearted, they would surely have dispersed from around you."
— Holy Qur'an

"A leader is a shield to the people"

"Be humble towards one another, so that no one oppresses or is condescending to another person."

The one who shows humility, God elevates in the estimation of the people."

"Advise me, O People"
— Muhammad before the Battle of Badr

"Allah's Messenger ﷺ fought [with us] in severe heat, struggling on our long journey, against the desert and the great strength of the enemy".

"O Messenger of Allah! Shall I tie [the camel's leg], or leave it loose and trust in Allah?" He said: "Tie it and put your trust in Allah."

"[It is] better for a leader to make a mistake in forgiving than to make it in punishing."

Seventh Century Arabia

Introduction

Assessing the leadership effectiveness of any historical figure is always problematical for two reasons. First, it is likely that the records of his or her actions were written by either acolytes or enemies, and are therefore imbued with bias and distortion; and second, it is hard to establish whether successes or failures can reasonably be attributed to the leader's qualities or actions, or whether myriad other factors and the actions of other people played significant roles in the way events unfolded.

Making sense of the leadership attributes of military leaders is especially difficult because of the tremendous loyalties, passions and hatreds that emerge during and after wars. The only leaders more difficult to analyse than military leaders are religious saints and prophets. Take the itinerant Jewish rabbi known as Jesus, for example. Even describing his profession and ethnicity in this mundane but factually correct fashion might inflame temper in a Christian believer who considers him not only divine, but perfect.

These epistemological challenges frame the enormity of the task of trying to say something objective, meaningful and accurate about the leadership of an individual such as the Islamic Prophet Muhammad. He was both a military leader involved in wars that created new power structures and a prophet who ushered in dramatically original ways of understanding monotheistic religion and its relationship with politics.

Scholars approaching Muhammad's life are at once confronted by the awkwardness that the very earliest extant sources that chronicle his life date from at least one hundred and forty years after his death in 632 CE, with almost no sources even of a fragmentary nature dating from within the first "silent" century or more. If his enemies or even neutral contemporary observers wrote accounts of his actions, they have not survived, with the exception of a few semi-coherent lines from Christian chroniclers in Greek, Syriac and Armenian that actually contradict the traditional Islamic narrative in places.[1] It is equally problematic that the only sources written in the eighth and ninth centuries CE with sufficient detail to support the construction of a narrative were written by acolytes who supposedly based them on earlier sources that are now lost or on oral traditions. This increases the possibility that the sources are imbued with bias and possibly include distortion or fabrication which were added to create, or at least strengthen, a single desired viewpoint.

This should not be read as doubt on the historicity of Muhammad. On the contrary, it is clear from the archaeological, numismatic and documentary records that Arab armies spilled out of the Arabian Peninsula in the seventh century CE, undertook substantial warfare in neighbouring regions, and established new cultural norms and a powerful polity in the name of the recently deceased Prophet Muhammad. One can only conclude, therefore, that he did live and the new religion of Islam grew from his teachings.

Scholars should not avoid trying to say something meaningful about Muhammad's life because of the possibility of subjectivity and bias in the sources and the fact that they date from the eighth and ninth centuries. Otherwise they would have to abandon trying to write about Alexander the Great, Julius Caesar, Jesus Christ, and many other historical figures. The key sources for their lives postdate the events by centuries, are equally problematic, and no less likely to contain subjectivity and bias. The earliest extant Greek source for Alexander's life, for example, is the *Bibliotheca historica*, written by Diodorus Siculus over 265 years after Alexander's death in 323 BCE. Even more inconvenient than this

Introduction

gap of 265 years is the fact that the oldest extant manuscript copy of the relevant section of the *Bibliotheca historica* (Book XVII) dates from the fifteenth century CE, over 1,500 years later.[2]

Even the best of the surprisingly few modern books on Muhammad's leadership are, in terms of leadership studies, somewhat old-fashioned in that they focus almost entirely on traits and attributes.[3] They say he was pious, honest, compassionate, tolerant, patient, fair, decisive and courageous; traits that made him a great leader. The books are well worth reading. Yet, with no disrespect to the authors, their logic rests on two erroneous deductive arguments: firstly, because the legacy of Muhammad's life is a flourishing world religion, we must consider him to have been a successful leader; and secondly, because he was both a very good man based on the aforementioned traits, and he was a successful leader, we must therefore deduce that he was a successful leader *because* he was very good man.

We can dismiss the first argument on the basis by itself that Jesus's lack of worldly success proves that a lasting religious legacy is not a sound criterion for judging a prophet's leadership. Jesus reportedly died a violent death after a short-lived ministry that, in his lifetime, secured him very few followers and no temporal power. Yet over two billion humans profess to follow his teachings. We are therefore left with the second argument. We might be able to look at its deductive reasoning in this fashion:

1. All successful leaders are good men or women. (First premise)
2. Muhammad was a good man. (Second premise)
3. Muhammad was a successful leader. (Third premise)
4. Therefore, Muhammad was a successful leader because he was a good man. (Conclusion)

Only one premise needs to be incorrect for the conclusion to be incorrect. The first premise is itself unsustainable. History reveals that very many deeply flawed, corrupt or wickedly cruel people —

including (by historical consensus) Julius Caesar, Genghis Khan, Napoleon, Stalin and Mao Zedong — have been very successful leaders. The second premise is sustainable, although debated by some critics. The third premise is equally sustainable, and with no debate. The conclusion itself therefore cannot be reached because of the inherent logical fallacy imbedded within the first premise. If we remove the first premise altogether, we are left only with correlation and no causality. That is, it can be true that a good person is a good leader. But it can be equally true that a bad person is a good leader. Likewise, it can be true that a good person is a bad leader, and equally true that a bad person is a bad leader. Thus, moral goodness in a leader does not *necessarily* cause leadership effectiveness, as an examination of the failed first premise shows.

This study avoids using traits and recourse to moral assessment as the primary basis of establishing Muhammad's leadership success. Instead, it attempts to analyse Muhammad's leadership ideas, methods, and related behaviour in order to ascertain whether his fascinating life can provide substantial and meaningful insights about the effectiveness of his strategic leadership. In order to do so, it will be necessary to draw information from two bodies of evidence dating from the ninth century CE: the six major Sunni collections of ahadith — أحاديث, "reports" or "traditions", the recorded sayings and practices of Muhammad — and the earliest extant books of *Sirah* (prophetic biography), especially Ibn Hisham's *Al-Sirah al-Nabawiyyah,* Al-Waqidi's *Kitab al-Maghazi* and Ibn Sa'd's *Kitab al-Tabaqat al-Kabir*.[4] It may be possible to use these sources to present a case study of Muhammad's life that will demystify some of strategic leadership's constituent processes.

This analysis is a work of history, not of *Fiqh* (Islamic jurisprudence). The author is a historian and strategic studies scholar, not a theologian or *faqih* (jurist). Using the established methodology of the historical discipline, this study attempts to reconstruct seventh-century events by interpreting, explaining and evaluating the earliest sources, all the while keeping issues of truth, objectivity and bias firmly in mind. It does not attempt to confront the *Fiqh* as it later evolved, but to reach beyond it, or more accurately *behind* it in time, to the historical events that once occurred in seventh-century Arabia. As a modest contribution to the *Sirah* literature and to strategic and leadership studies, it attempts to analyse thematically rather than describe chronologically certain practices from within Muhammad's twenty-three years as a leader.

NOTE: in the ahadith one finds after Muhammad's name or title the words "prayers and peace be upon him" (represented in calligraphy as ﷺ). This calligraphy is not used throughout this book except in direct quotations from ahadith.

Theocentric Leadership

Perhaps the ideal starting point is to examine how Muhammad understood leadership because this will logically frame the way his inputs and outcomes can be analysed. Scholars can find examples of both his understanding and practice in the ahadith. In the eighth and ninth centuries CE, particularly in Iraq and Persia, certain scholars began to collect, evaluate, organise and publish collections of sayings and actions attributed to Muhammad by chains of narrators leading back to companions who had purportedly heard or seen those statements or deeds. Despite the passage of at least a century and a half since the Prophet's death, and the malleability and imperfection of human memory even in societies with strong oral traditions, voluminous collections of those reports began to form the basis of much of Islamic jurisprudence and philosophy. Indeed, within the Islamic Shari'ah, the ahadith are considered the second most important and reliable source, surpassed only by the Qur'an.

One cannot accept every hadith or even a majority as entirely reliable — meaning a perfectly verbatim record of what Muhammad said or did 1,400 years ago — and no Islamic scholars have said they should be accepted as such. The scholarly consensus is that each hadith should be considered carefully regarding its *isnad* (إسناد, the chain of transmission) *and* the *matn* (متن, the consistency and plausibility of its content). Merely having a sound chain will not render an inconsistent or implausible hadith reliable; nor will having a consistent or plausible statement that lacks a sound chain.

Both need to be present, and this book builds only upon ahadith that satisfy this criterion and are considered reliable by scholarly consensus. It does not draw upon any ahadith considered by this author or by other scholars to be fraudulent or unusably unreliable, even though this means leaving out many of the ahadith on Muhammad's leadership that are now popular among Muslims (such as "The leader is the servant of the people").

As a man of deep faith, Muhammad embraced and taught a theocentric understanding of leadership; that is, he believed that ultimately God chooses and puts in place all leaders, regardless of the specific procedure of a person's appointment to a leadership role within a community or army.

Muhammad also believed that the main responsibility of a leader is to act as a *shepherd*. Reliable ahadith confirm that he saw human interactions in terms of God-given responsibilities to provide safety, guidance and care. In *Sunan Abu Dawud*, for example, we find this illuminating hadith:

> 'Abdullah ibn 'Umar narrated that the Messenger of Allah ﷺ said: Each of you is a shepherd [راعِي, *ra'i*] and will be asked [by God about how you provide care]. The leader of the people [أمير, *emir*] is a shepherd who will be asked about his treatment of the flock; a man is a shepherd who will be asked about the treatment of the members of his household; the woman is a shepherd who will be asked about her treatment of the husband's house and children; and a servant is a shepherd who will be asked about his treatment of his master's possessions. Each of you is a shepherd responsible for a flock.[5]

We know that in Classical Arabic the word مَسْئُولً means to provide an account of one's conduct, because the Qur'an has this verse:

$$\text{وَلَا تَقْرَبُواْ مَالَ الْيَتِيمِ إِلَّا بِالَّتِي هِيَ أَحْسَنُ حَتَّى يَبْلُغَ أَشُدَّهُ وَأَوْفُواْ بِالْعَهْدِ إِنَّ الْعَهْدَ كَانَ مَسْؤُولًا.}$$

Do not come near to the orphan's property, except to improve it, until he attains his maturity; and fulfil your responsibilities, for [the taking care of] responsibilities will be enquired of [مَسْئُولًا by Allah on the Day of Judgment].[6]

And this verse:

$$\text{وَلَا تَقْفُ مَا لَيْسَ لَكَ بِهِ عِلْمٌ إِنَّ السَّمْعَ وَالْبَصَرَ وَالْفُؤَادَ كُلُّ أُولَئِكَ كَانَ عَنْهُ مَسْؤُولًا.}$$

And do not pursue that of which you have no knowledge; surely about the hearing and the sight and the heart, [you] shall be questioned.[7]

This reveals that a leader is a shepherd both responsible *and accountable* for the safety and protection of the flock, a position reinforced by another of Muhammad's statements:

> Ibn 'Umar saw a shepherd with some sheep situated very badly although he saw that there was a better place. He told him, "Woe to you, shepherd! Move them! I heard the Messenger of Allah ﷺ say, "Every shepherd is responsible for his flock.""[8]

The distinctly biblical imagery associated with shepherding is not coincidental. Muhammad believed that his prophethood was essentially the same as the calling bestowed on Abraham, Moses, David, Jesus and other prophets, and he saw shepherding flocks as a common activity of all the prophets:

> Narrated Jabir ibn 'Abdullah: We were with Allah's Messenger ﷺ picking fruit from the 'Arak trees, and Allah's Messenger ﷺ said, "Pick the black fruit, for it is the best." The companions asked, "Were you a shepherd?" He replied, "There was no prophet who was not a shepherd."[9]

One might feel tempted to read this hadith purely metaphorically; that Muhammad was saying that all prophets were *like* shepherds because of their burden of responsibility for others. That is, they guarded and protected their flocks. This meaning is undoubtedly embedded within Muhammad's statement. Yet we have other ahadith that reveal that he also meant that he and other prophets had literally shepherded animals.

> 'Abda ibn Hazn said, "The people of camels and the people of sheep vied with one another for glory. The Prophet ﷺ said, "Musa [Moses] was sent as a shepherd. Da'ud [David] was sent as a shepherd. I was sent, and I used to herd sheep for my people at Ajyad."[10]

Similarly:

> Abu Huraira narrated that the Prophet ﷺ said, "Allah did not send any prophet except those who shepherded sheep." His companions asked him, "Did you do the same?" The Prophet ﷺ replied, "Yes, I used to shepherd the sheep of the people of Mecca for a little payment."[11]

In saying this, he wanted to explain that God had prepared all prophets for leadership roles by first teaching them to care for sheep, a responsibility that involves dedication, calmness and great patience. Certainly he believed that the quiet, tranquil and patient nature of shepherding, unlike the rearing of horses or camels, increases the calmness of the shepherd.

> Abu Huraira narrated that Allah's Messenger ﷺ said, "The source of disbelief is in the east. Pride and arrogance are in the owners of horses and camels, and those crude desert people who are too busy with their camels; while tranquility is the characteristic of those with sheep."[12]

One might assume, therefore, that if calmness is a quality wanted in a leader, Muhammad would enjoy seeing women in leadership positions. Yet a hadith seems to suggest, if read uncritically, that he believed that women should not in fact assume political leadership roles.

> Abu Bakrah said: "Allah protected me with something that I heard from the Messenger of Allah ﷺ. When Khosrow [King of the Sasanian Empire] died, he said: 'Who have they appointed as his successor?' They said: 'His daughter' [presumably meaning Queen Būrāndukht[13]]. He said: 'No people will ever prosper who entrust their leadership to a woman.'"[14]

Given that this assertion contradicts with the Queen of Sheba's positive description in the Qur'an as a strong, wise and independent leader,[15] and that Abu Bakrah is not seen as a reliable narrator,[16] scholars are not agreed on the reliability and applicability of the hadith. Although Islamic jurists can make a case that God has chosen certain forms of religious and military leadership to be undertaken by men — for example as imams in mosques and as generals in armies[17] — one simply cannot make a case that women are excluded from political and communal leadership roles.

The Qur'an reveals that, in Islam, divine appointment is the basis of all leadership; that Allah gives leadership roles to people of his choice, and that this appointment explains both good and bad leaders. Speaking of Abraham and his prophetic offspring, the Qur'an says:

$$\text{وَجَعَلْنَاهُمْ أَئِمَّةً يَهْدُونَ بِأَمْرِنَا وَأَوْحَيْنَا إِلَيْهِمْ فِعْلَ الْخَيْرَاتِ وَإِقَامَ الصَّلَاةِ وَإِيتَاءَ الزَّكَاةِ وَكَانُوا لَنَا عَابِدِينَ}$$

And We made them leaders [*a'immatan*] who guide by Our command. And We inspired in them the doing of good deeds, the establishment of prayer, and the giving of charity; and they were worshippers of Us.[18]

Similarly, the Qur'an says in another chapter:

$$\text{وَجَعَلْنَا مِنْهُمْ أَئِمَّةً يَهْدُونَ بِأَمْرِنَا لَمَّا صَبَرُوا وَكَانُوا بِآيَاتِنَا يُوقِنُونَ}$$

And We made from among them [the Children of Israel] leaders guiding by Our command when they were patient and had sure faith in Our signs.[19]

Some leaders were clearly not appointed for their goodness, and the Qur'an gives examples of the term *imam* (إمام, leader) applying even to wicked opponents of Islam:

$$\text{وَإِن نَّكَثُوا أَيْمَانَهُم مِّن بَعْدِ عَهْدِهِمْ وَطَعَنُوا فِي دِينِكُمْ فَقَاتِلُوا أَئِمَّةَ الْكُفْرِ إِنَّهُمْ لَا أَيْمَانَ لَهُمْ لَعَلَّهُمْ يَنتَهُونَ}$$

Fight against the leaders of the unbelievers [the polytheists in Mecca] if they violate their peace treaty with you and revile your faith, to force them to stop their aggression against you. You do not have to stay bound to such a treaty.[20]

Similarly,

$$\text{وَجَعَلْنَاهُمْ أَئِمَّةً يَدْعُونَ إِلَى النَّارِ وَيَوْمَ الْقِيَامَةِ لَا يُنصَرُونَ}$$

We made them [Egyptian leaders at the time of the exodus] the kinds of leaders who invite people to the fire [of Hell] and who will receive no help on the Day of Judgment.²¹

The key action associated with the word إمام is clearly the provision of guidance, as another verse makes clear by using the word for divine scriptures themselves:

وَمِن قَبْلِهِ كِتَابُ مُوسَى إِمَاماً وَرَحْمَةً وَهَذَا كِتَابٌ مُصَدِّقٌ لِّسَاناً عَرَبِيّاً لِّيُنذِرَ الَّذِينَ ظَلَمُوا وَبُشْرَى لِلْمُحْسِنِينَ

Before this [Qur'an], the Book of Moses was a guide and a blessing [إِمَاماً وَرَحْمَةً]. This Book confirms [its truth] in the Arabic language so that it may warn the unjust people and give glad news to those who do good.²²

That does not mean that followers of Islam are compelled to comply with the guidance of *any* leaders. The Qur'an says that "believers" must "not obey sinners and unbelievers" (وَلَا تُطِعْ مِنْهُمْ آثِماً أَوْ كَفُوراً)²³ but must instead obey morally good leaders:

يَا أَيُّهَا الَّذِينَ آمَنُوا أَطِيعُوا اللَّهَ وَأَطِيعُوا الرَّسُولَ وَأُوْلِي الأَمْرِ مِنكُمْ فَإِن تَنَازَعْتُمْ فِي شَيْءٍ فَرُدُّوهُ إِلَى اللَّهِ وَالرَّسُولِ إِن كُنتُمْ تُؤْمِنُونَ بِاللَّهِ وَالْيَوْمِ الآخِرِ ذَلِكَ خَيْرٌ وَأَحْسَنُ تَأْوِيلاً

O you believers, obey Allah, the Messenger, and those with command among you. If you have faith in Allah and the Day of Judgment, refer to Allah and the Messenger concerning matters in which you differ. That is a more virtuous and better way of settling differences.²⁴

Understanding Authority

The Qur'an is clear that people within the community of belief are required to submit to the direction of not only the Prophet, but also of "those with command among you" (وَأُوْلِي الأَمْرِ مِنكُمْ). A hadith suggests that this verse initially related to Muhammad's appointment of 'Abdullah ibn Hudhafa ibn Qais ibn 'Adi to lead a detachment of troops on a raid.[25] In other words, God was saying that the Prophet's many appointees as leaders were also entitled to total obedience.

The trilateral root *hamza mīm rā* (أ م ر) occurs 248 times in the Quran, most commonly (166 times) as the noun *amr* (أَمْر) and (77 times) as form I verb *amara* (أَمَرَ), both referring to "command" or "order".[26] The triliteral root *ṭā wāw 'ayn* (ط و ع) occurs 129 times in the Quran, most commonly (72 times) as the form IV verb *aṭā'a* (أَطَاعَ), which simply means "to obey". It is thus clear that leadership, according to Qur'an, involves a relationship between leaders whom God empowered to command and order, and the led, who must obey those leaders.

The Qur'anic revelation is clear that prophets' authority came from God: "We sent no messenger but to be obeyed, by the will of Allah." (وَمَا أَرْسَلْنَا مِن رَّسُولٍ إِلاَّ لِيُطَاعَ بِإِذْنِ اللّهِ).[27] Jesus was empowered in this fashion and was to be obeyed. In *Surah al-Imran* we thus find:

وَمُصَدِّقاً لِّمَا بَيْنَ يَدَيَّ مِنَ التَّوْرَاةِ وَلِأُحِلَّ لَكُم بَعْضَ الَّذِي حُرِّمَ عَلَيْكُمْ وَجِئْتُكُم بِآيَةٍ مِّن رَّبِّكُمْ فَاتَّقُواْ اللّهَ وَأَطِيعُونِ

And [I Jesus have come] confirming what was before me of the Torah and to make lawful for you some of what was forbidden to you. And I have come to you with a sign from your Lord, so fear Allah and obey me.[28]

This of course echoes what we find in the New Testament, which quotes Jesus instructing his followers, "If you love me, obey my commands" (Ἐὰν ἀγαπᾶτέ με, τὰς ἐντολὰς τὰς ἐμὰς τηρήσετε), and asking, "Why do you call me 'Lord, Lord,' and not do what I tell you?" (Τί δέ με καλεῖτε, Κύριε κύριε, καὶ οὐ ποιεῖτε ἃ λέγω).[29] One should not be surprised to find Jesus demanding obedience. It was a privilege given to Hebrew prophets before him, as the Torah reveals: "I will raise up for them from among their own people a prophet like yourself, in whose mouth I will put My words and who will speak to them all that I command; and anybody who fails to obey the words he speaks in My name, I Myself will call to account." (רֹשֵׁא ,יָרַבְּד-לֹאֵ עַמְשִׁי-אל רֹשֵׁא שׁיאָה ,הָיָהְו .רַבֵּדְי ,יִכֹנָאֵ שׁרֹדְאָ שֶׁרֹדִי ,וּמַעְמ).[30]

The Qur'an likewise directly equates obedience to the Prophet Muhammad with obedience to God: "Whoever obeys the Messenger surely obeys God" (مَنْ يُطِعِ الرَّسُولَ فَقَدْ أَطَاعَ اللَّـهَ).[31]

We also find this explicitly stated in ahadith which quote Muhammad stating: "Whoever obeys me, obeys Allah, and whoever disobeys me, disobeys Allah, and whoever obeys the leader I appoint, obeys me, and whoever disobeys him, disobeys me."[32]

One can therefore see that a prophet is in a unique leadership position. Even more so than a senior military officer in today's world — whose formal status and position within the hierarchy grant him significant direct authority over those in his or her command and the ability to initiate formal measures against anyone who disobeys a lawful instruction — a prophet can demand total obedience to any command, with divine punishment going to anyone who might disobey. As the Qur'an states:

وَمَن يَعْصِ اللَّهَ وَرَسُولَهُ وَيَتَعَدَّ حُدُودَهُ يُدْخِلْهُ نَاراً خَالِداً فِيهَا وَلَهُ عَذَابٌ مُهِينٌ.

And whoever disobeys Allah and his Messenger and [thus] transgresses limits, will be admitted to the fire wherein they will live forever, suffering a humiliating punishment.[33]

This is not to say that even prophets are always obeyed. Sometimes Muhammad found himself being disobeyed, much to his sadness. For example, during the Battle of Uhud in March 625, members of his army disobeyed his explicit instructions by leaving a tactically crucial hill, thus causing a military defeat.[34] The Qur'an directly addresses this disobedience:

وَلَقَدْ صَدَقَكُمُ اللَّهُ وَعْدَهُ إِذْ تَحُسُّونَهُم بِإِذْنِهِ حَتَّى إِذَا فَشِلْتُمْ وَتَنَازَعْتُمْ فِي الأَمْرِ وَعَصَيْتُم مِّن بَعْدِ مَا أَرَاكُم مَّا تُحِبُّونَ مِنكُم مَّن يُرِيدُ الدُّنْيَا وَمِنكُم مَّن يُرِيدُ الآخِرَةَ ثُمَّ صَرَفَكُمْ عَنْهُمْ لِيَبْتَلِيَكُمْ وَلَقَدْ عَفَا عَنكُمْ وَاللَّهُ ذُو فَضْلٍ عَلَى الْمُؤْمِنِينَ.

Allah certainly fulfilled His promise to you when you were fighting the unbelievers, by His permission. Even after We showed you what you wanted, you began to lose courage, started quarreling with each other, and disobeyed Allah's orders. Some of you want worldly gains and others of you want rewards in the hereafter. Then He let you face defeat in order to test you. However, He forgave you. Allah is Gracious to the believers.[35]

Another Qur'anic verse exhorted Muhammad not to be disheartened, but rather to forgive the disobedient at Uhud and to stay gentle with them:

فَبِمَا رَحْمَةٍ مِّنَ اللَّهِ لِنتَ لَهُمْ وَلَوْ كُنتَ فَظّاً غَلِيظَ الْقَلْبِ لاَنفَضُّواْ مِنْ

حَوْلِكَ فَاعْفُ عَنْهُمْ وَاسْتَغْفِرْ لَهُمْ وَشَاوِرْهُمْ فِي الْأَمْرِ فَإِذَا عَزَمْتَ فَتَوَكَّلْ عَلَى اللَّهِ إِنَّ اللَّهَ يُحِبُّ الْمُتَوَكِّلِينَ.

It was through Allah's mercy that you [Muhammad] have been able to deal with them so gently. If you had been stern and hard-hearted, they would surely have dispersed from around you. Forgive them and ask Allah to forgive them and consult with them [again] on affairs. Then, when you reach a decision, trust Allah. God loves those who trust Him.[36]

In seventh century Arabia, obedience to leaders was expressed via a formal pledge of allegiance called *bay'a*, a word which derives from the Arabic root *by'*, which denotes both buying and selling. This pledge, therefore, was originally a transaction ratified by a handshake of the parties involved.[37] It involved two-way responsibilities, with the leader implicitly or explicitly agreeing to lead fairly and wisely and possibly bestow largesse, and the other party agreeing to obey instructions and offer required service and any stipulated taxes or tribute.

The concept that obeying Muhamad was the same as obeying God is evident in the sources. The Qur'an informs Muhammad, who in March 628 CE personally accepted with hand clasps the pledge of his followers (immediately preceding the Treaty of Hudaybiyyah), that:

فَبِمَا رَحْمَةٍ مِّنَ اللَّهِ لِنتَ لَهُمْ وَلَوْ كُنتَ فَظًّا غَلِيظَ الْقَلْبِ لَانفَضُّواْ مِنْ حَوْلِكَ فَاعْفُ عَنْهُمْ وَاسْتَغْفِرْ لَهُمْ

وَشَاوِرْهُمْ فِي الْأَمْرِ فَإِذَا عَزَمْتَ فَتَوَكَّلْ عَلَى اللَّهِ إِنَّ اللَّهَ يُحِبُّ الْمُتَوَكِّلِينَ.

Those who pledge allegiance to you, it is to Allah that they pledge. The hand of God is above [i.e., clasps] their hands. As for those who break their pledge, they do so only against their own souls. Those who fulfill their promise to God will receive a great reward.[38]

Thus, a pledge of allegiance with Muhammad was more than merely a transactional civil matter; it was also deeply religiously binding. Historian Ella Landau-Tasseron reveals its seriousness:

> "[Exchanging] pledges with the Prophet (which was done by a hand clasp) was tantamount to a bayʻa with Allah and constituted an unequivocal commitment to Him. … Such perception of the bayʻa elucidates the Islamic viewpoint that it is irrevocable. Withdrawing a bayʻa exchanged with the Prophet on behalf of Allah amounted to apostasy, which, like unbelief, is punishable by death."[39]

There are literally hundreds of ahadith that convey the seriousness with which both Muhammad and his companions and followers regarded the bayʻa.

Yet one should not mistake this formal pledge as an inflexible fear-based substitute for good leadership; that Muhammad's followers feared him and the consequences of breaking their pledge and only obeyed him because of that fear. On the contrary, as will be shown below, Muhammad possessed remarkable gifts of inspiration and persuasion. His followers served him with dedication and tremendous respect and affection.

Even the bayʻa sworn to him was gentler in intent than the rather ominous-sounding Qur'anic verses above suggest if read without context. It contains a "do your best" type of qualifier. For example, in *Sahih al-Bukhari* we find this hadith: "Whenever we gave the pledge of allegiance to Allah's Messenger ﷺ to listen to and obey him, he used to say to us, 'for as much as you can.'"[40] Similarly, when Muhammad entered Mecca in 630 CE at the head of an army of ten thousand and occupied his old hometown without bloodshed, promptly forgiving its citizens for eight years of fighting and many years before that of ridicule and persecution, he duly asked for their collective pledge of fealty. In front of the Ka'ba, the holy house in Mecca's center, he accepted their promise to listen to him and obey him, "as best they could."[41]

The pledge itself ordinarily followed a formula involving — along with the clasping of hands — a promise to listen to the Prophet and to obey his instructions, to associate no gods with Allah and to live well according to Islamic teachings, to be good to other Muslims, and perhaps also to undertake a particular task, such as to emigrate to Medina or to participate in a raid or battle on behalf of the Islamic polity.

The phrase "to listen to and obey" the Prophet (عَلَى السَّمْعِ وَالطَّاعَةِ) occurs in virtually every hadith discussing bay'a and places upon the follower an active, rather than passive, responsibility to try to understand Muhammad's intentions.

Whether one liked a tasking or not, the subordinate had to obey.[42] Aware that some leaders might rely on this concept of obedience to compel subordinates to do unethical things, Muhammad explained that trying to understand what one was told to do and why (the listening) was as important as carrying out the instruction (the obedience), with critical thinking being necessary to determine whether the instruction was a righteous task.[43]

Muhammad was gentle and flexible when he recognised sometimes that a greater good might be accomplished by releasing someone from a vow. When a young man happened to tell him that his pledge to emigrate with him (presumably to Medina) had made his parents cry, he humanely said: "Go back to them, and make them smile just as you had made them weep."[44]

Obedience was also unrequired if any instruction violated the principles of Islam or even of commonsense (understood to be what is well known to be good[45]). For example, after swearing to obey a troop leader appointed by the Prophet, certain soldiers were slow to build the fire the leader had demanded. He then became enraged, ordered them to build a fire and throw themselves into it. They duly built the fire but then, before throwing themselves into it, demurred and said to the leader: "We followed the Prophet ﷺ to escape from the fire [i.e. Hell]. How should we enter it now?" The fire subsided and the commander's temper cooled. When Muhammad heard of this, he said, "If they had entered it [the fire] they would never have come out of it [i.e., they would have remained in hellfire], for obedience is required only in what is good."[46]

One can also imagine the enthusiasm that accompanied pledging obedience to Muhammad. Breaking the pledge would evoke God's wrath, but, conversely, keeping it would bring spiritual rewards, including Paradise (described in the verse quoted above as "a great reward"[47]) and even success and blessings in this life. We thus find even powerful men pledging allegiance with a promise of earthly benefit. We have a record, for example, of 'Amr ibn al-'As, a Meccan antagonist of Muhammad, finally swearing allegiance to Muhammad "on the condition that my past sins be pardoned and that he [Muhammad] give me an active part in affairs, and he did so."[48] 'Amr went on to become a great Islamic hero who led the Muslim conquest of Egypt and served as its governor in 640–646 and 658–664 CE.

Reward for obedience was not unusual. After all, the Qur'an is clear that loyalty and obedience to the Prophet would bring earthly benefit. Regarding those who pledged their bay'a at Hudaybiyyah, the Qur'an says:

لَقَدْ رَضِيَ اللَّهُ عَنِ الْمُؤْمِنِينَ إِذْ يُبَايِعُونَكَ تَحْتَ الشَّجَرَةِ فَعَلِمَ مَا فِي قُلُوبِهِمْ فَأَنزَلَ السَّكِينَةَ عَلَيْهِمْ وَأَثَابَهُمْ فَتْحاً قَرِيباً.

وَمَغَانِمَ كَثِيرَةً يَأْخُذُونَهَا وَكَانَ اللَّهُ عَزِيزاً حَكِيماً.

Certainly, Allah was pleased with the believers when they pledged allegiance to you under the tree, and He knew what was in their hearts, so He sent down tranquility on them and rewarded them with an imminent victory, and much [war] booty that they will capture. Allah is Almighty and Wise.[49]

Consultative Leadership

In the aforementioned Qur'anic verse from *Surah al-Imran*, which has God praise Muhammad for being "gentle" and not "stern and hard-hearted" despite suffering a military defeat caused by the disobedience of some of his soldiers, God tells Muhammad to "forgive them and ask Allah to forgive them". Remarkably, rather than imposing any form of punishment or exclusion upon the disobedient, God then tells Muhammad to deal with them in this fashion: "consult with them on [i.e., about] affairs. Then, when you reach a decision, trust Allah."

Shura (شُورَىٰ) is a form of peer consultation and participatory decision-making found among Arab leaders at all levels. Its origins predate the coming of Islam.[50] It involves the discussion of problems or issues by peer groups with a view to determining a way forward through dialogue, respectful debate and collective decision-making. It seems ideally suited to tribal societies, where members of different tribes can meet as peers to decide matters of mutual concern, or where elders within a tribe can meet to provide advice or act as agents of accountability for a chief.

The Qur'an presents Shura as an important social function for *all* people everywhere and as a necessary means of gaining wisdom. It places Shura alongside prayer and charity as essential human behaviour:

وَالَّذِينَ اسْتَجَابُوا لِرَبِّهِمْ وَأَقَامُوا الصَّلَاةَ وَأَمْرُهُمْ شُورَىٰ بَيْنَهُمْ وَمِمَّا رَزَقْنَاهُمْ يُنفِقُونَ.

> And those who respond to their Lord and keep up prayer, and [manage] their affairs through consultation [شُورَى], and who spend from what We have given them, [will receive reward from Allah].[51]

This sums up the highly consultative style of leadership that Muhammad tried steadfastly to utilise throughout his twenty-three years of leadership. Despite having a community solemnly sworn to obey him by way of bay'a, which he took very seriously, he avoided running roughshod over others and understood that people around him possessed vantage points, ideas and insights that might help him to make stronger decisions than those he could make by himself. They also had dignity, which could be strengthened by inclusion.

Muhammad liked good ideas, whomever they came from. He therefore routinely asked for advice, listened dispassionately, praised the contributors, reflected, decided, and then trusted in God. It was not just a process of listening; of gaining advice. As often as he could he sought consensus, to which he acquiesced, and clearly enjoyed participatory decision-making.

Aware that he was both a divinely appointed prophet and an ordinary man — "But I am [only] human" (إِنَّمَا أَنَا بَشَرٌ) was a phrase he often used[52] — he remained psychologically able to juggle this inherent tension, and never confused his own thoughts with those of God that came as revelation. As such, he made it clear that he wanted input from others on matters that he was deciding himself, as opposed to divine direction communicated from heaven. He therefore created an open and safe environment in which people could debate or even contradict him without being seen as disrespectful or disloyal. Far from being an omniscient autocrat, he was an inclusive and consultative decision-maker whose own ideas could be discussed, improved upon, or even constructively criticised.

Indeed, the two earliest extant biographies, Ibn Hisham's

Al-Sirah al-Nabawiyyah and Al-Waqidi's *Kitab al-Maghazi*, reveal that before every major event in his life, including the Hijra (هِجْرَة, emigration) from Mecca to Medina in 622 CE and all the subsequent raids and battles, he consulted with his trusted confidantes. For instance, before Islam's first great victory, the Battle of Badr on 13 March 624, the Prophet first discussed options with his inner circle, asking whether they should withdraw or proceed. "Advise me, O People," he said. They seemed to support advancing to battle, and Muhammad was especially heartened when Al-Miqdad ibn 'Amr promised that, contrary to Prophet Moses' people not wanting to fight with him, Muhammad could count on his followers' total support.[53] Muhammad did not stop there. He then consulted with the Ansar, the citizens of Medina who had welcomed him into their midst. "Advise me," he requested, receiving the positive advice that they would honour their bay'a pledge to "listen to and obey" and that they would indeed fight if he wished to proceed.

The Battle of Badr involved another remarkable example of Muhammad actively seeking and taking advice before making a decision. When he led his force of 313 soldiers to the sandy valley of Badr, southwest of Medina, he proposed establishing his camp, and thus his fighting line, at a certain location. He then asked his companions for advice regarding his choice. A member of the Khazraj tribe, Al-Hubab ibn al-Mundhir, asked, "O Messenger of Allah, have you given thought to this site? Has Allah told you that this is the right site? Because if He has it is not for us to encourage you or deter you regarding it. Or is it your decision as a tactic of war?"[54]

This might seem impertinent to modern ears, but Muhammad took no offence. He replied: "It is my decision as a tactic of war." Al-Hubab ibn al-Mundhir then spoke the truth plainly to the man he saw as God's messenger: "This is certainly not a good site."[55] He explained his rationale. They should set up camp near the farthest wells, which they could exploit for fresh water, while denying the enemy those and the closer wells. Unperturbed that he had not thought of this, and not stung by the criticism of his own choice, Muhammad readily agreed to Al-Hubab's advice. He ordered the camp moved to the specified wells, and the next day enjoyed a dramatic victory over a significantly larger force.

Al-Hubab ibn al-Mundhir features often and positively throughout the earliest biographies of Muhammad, and, interestingly, he once again corrected the Prophet regarding the positioning of troops. At the beginning of the Battle of Ta'if in February 630, six years after the Battle of Badr, Muhammad positioned his camp close to the city walls. Once again Al-Hubab challenged the decision, telling him: "O Allah's Messenger, we are really close to the fortress. If this decision was because of Allah's command, we will submit, but if it's your own judgment you should move back from the wall."[56] They were within the defenders' arrow reach, he explained, and were suffering injuries.

One might think that Muhammad had put up with this type of correction six years earlier because he was then a novice military commander, and that he had now, after having won many battles and conquered Mecca, come to see himself as sufficiently expert that such a correction would be annoying. Not only that, but he was a divinely appointed prophet who did not, as the Qur'an says, "speak from his own desires, but only from a revelation brought forth." (وَمَا يَنطِقُ عَنِ الْهَوَىٰ. إِنْ هُوَ إِلَّا وَحْيٌ يُوحَىٰ)[57] Yet the sources reveal no rancour. The humble Muhammad merely asked Al-Hubab to find a better location for them to withdraw to, which he did.

The sources reveal that the siege of Ta'if did not progress well, and losses were mounting after eighteen difficult days, so Muhammad sought the advice of Nawfal ibn Mu'awiya al-Dili, an accomplished warrior. Should they persist, or break off the siege? Nawfal gave an eloquent reply, explaining that Muhammad had already forced "the fox into its hole" and that if Muhammad persisted success would eventually come, but if he chose to withdraw, the fox could cause no harm.[58] Muhammad liked the advice, reflected, and ordered a withdrawal. Other advisors bitterly complained. Having spent over two weeks seeking victory, they thought this was bad advice. Victory was likely to be imminent. Muhammad remained patient, and agreed with the majority view that they should try one more assault the next morning.[59] It duly failed, with high casualties, so when Muhammad ordered the withdrawal the companions who had previously demanded another attempt were actually relieved.

It may seem that consultation and inclusive decision-making occurred only during wartime, but this was not the case. Even on social and cultural matters Muhammad liked to engage with people and hear views, routinely publicly praising the view of the person who initiated the discussion or whose opinion eventually prevailed, even if it had differed from his own. He delighted in good ideas, and made sure everyone knew who had advanced them, without claiming them as his own. He believed that credit should go to whom it was due.

Even the *adhan* (أَذَان), the Islamic call to prayer made five times a day, which now seems so integral to Islam that it must have originated in divine revelation, grew from very human discussions and widespread input. Some suggested that a flag could be raised prior to the prayer, but when it was pointed out that a flag could be obscured by trees or buildings, and could not be seen during darkness, others suggested the blowing of a horn, as the Jews did, but this was challenged on the basis that no-one would know who was calling them to prayer: the Jews or the Muslims. The same challenge applied to the ringing of a bell, as the Christians did. Finally, a group of others suggested that the human voice, with a specific Islamic invocation, would both honour God and be distinct from the other faith communities. The group accepted the idea. Yet the specifics still needed to be agreed upon. One companion, 'Abdullah ibn Zayd, informed them that he had a dream in which someone taught him the wording and intonation of would become the approved *adhan*.[60] 'Umar ibn al-Khattab advised that he had dreamed the same dream. They all agreed to it. Because the Prophet believed that Bilal ibn Rabah, a freed slave, had a stronger voice (one hadith says that it was actually because 'Abdullah was unwell that day[61]), he asked 'Abdullah to teach the words to Bilal, who added from his own ingenuity the line "*Al-salatu khairum min al-nawm*" (ٱلصَّلَاةُ خَيْرٌ مِنَ ٱلنَّوْمِ, "The prayer is better than sleep") to the call for the dawn prayer.[62] The *adhan* was thus a thoroughly collective decision merely ratified by a pleased Muhammad.

This is not to say that Muhammad always simply deferred to advice. He believed that only someone with a reputation as trustworthy should be consulted or listened to.[63] The "ignorant" should be avoided, because "they give advice based on opinions that will lead others astray."[64]

Sometimes he listened to advice and then stuck to his original inclination, especially if the advice came outside of a Shura meeting where he could hear all sides of an issue being debated. For example, at the Battle of Badr one of his companions offered corrective advice about the way Muhammad had arranged his warriors into lines. He used a similar formula: "O Allah's Messenger, if this came to you through revelation, then so be it, but if not, I think you should …"[65] With no Shura group to comment on this advice, and no consensus to seek, the Prophet gently dismissed it. It is significant, of course, that he had created an open environment in which his comrades felt free to offer advice even though they acknowledged him as a divinely chosen prophet.

The most famous example of Muhammad making a major decision after taking advice relates to the so-called Battle of the Trench. The Quraysh tribe of Mecca had allied with other tribes to form a substantial military force which advanced upon Muhammad's city Medina in March 627 with the intention of killing Muhammad, or at least ending his influence, once and for all. When Muhammad learned that a powerful force would soon reach Medina, he assembled his inner circle to learn their assessments and hear their views on how best to respond. The chronicler al-Waqidi says that this has been Muhammad's practice: "The Messenger of Allah consulted frequently with them on matters of war."[66]

Muhammad was himself not inclined to lead the army out of the city to fight a pitched battle in the Uhud valley. He had unsuccessfully done exactly that a year earlier, having at that time agreed to the consensus view of his confidantes over his own clearly expressed preference during a lengthy Shura.[67] This time, significant debate occurred, doubtless because of fear of a repeat failure.

Salman al-Farasi, a Persian convert to Islam, then spoke up, advising Muhammad that in Persia they had responded to the threat of cavalry attack with entrenchment; that is, by digging a trench that horses could neither jump across not climb out of. A trench across the valley neck leading into Medina would prevent the enemy entering. This tactic had never been used in Arabia, yet Salman's suggestion "pleased the Muslims," and thus earned Muhammad's favour.[68]

Seeing consensus, he agreed and ordered the digging of Salman's trench.[69] Muhammad even toiled in the strenuous digging, showing his followers that he would not ask of them something he would not do himself. The trench proved impassable to the enemy force, which was logistically weak and could not sustain its offensive in the insufferable heat, and thus saved the Muslim polity.

There is only one known major case of Muhammad opposing the view of his Shura. This occurred in 628 CE when he led 1,400 Muslims from Medina to Mecca in order to undertake an 'Umrah, or "lesser" pilgrimage. The Quraysh tribe in Mecca sent representatives to advise Muhammad, then camped at Hudaybiyyah outside Mecca, that — despite the Muslims wearing pilgrim garments and carrying only a few weapons for sacrificing animals and deterring bandits — they would not be allowed to proceed to Mecca. After negotiations, Muhammad chose to resolve the matter through diplomacy rather than warfare, and he authorised the drafting of a treaty between him and the Quraysh.

At each stage of the negotiation process he consulted with

his advisers, but many of them felt that he was acting weakly by promising them an 'Umrah he could not deliver and that the treaty itself was unworthy of a prophet. They told him so; bluntly. Even 'Umar ibn al-Khattab, one of Muhammad's closest confidantes and later a political successor, vehemently criticised the Prophet's decision to accept a negotiated settlement, all the more after Suhayl ibn 'Amr, a very skilled statesman and mediator representing the Quraysh, would not allow the attributes of Allah, or any reference to Muhammad being God's Messenger, to remain in the treaty text.[70]

Displaying enormous moral courage, the Prophet went against the consensus of his advisers, and entered into the treaty with his former enemy, agreeing that a state of peace would exist for ten years and that the Muslims would make their pilgrimage a year later.

It may have required Muhammad to submit to condescending and ignoble treatment in the short term, but he was sufficiently astute to see what his advisors could not: that he could swallow his pride that day, and surrender the short-term goal of performing pilgrimage in Mecca, in order to secure the far greater long-term political rewards: Quraysh's recognition of him as a negotiating equal (that is, that he was no longer merely a rebel, but was a legitimate leader of a recognised polity that was now accorded the status of a major tribe); a decade of peace with his intransigent foe; and the right henceforth to make pilgrimages.

If Muhammad was hurt by his close comrades' anger and opposition, he did not let that pain damage relations for long. After a Qur'anic revelation confirmed that the treaty was a "manifest victory" from God (إِنَّا فَتَحْنَا لَكَ فَتْحاً مُبِيناً)[71], Muhammad fully reconciled with 'Umar and the other dissenters.[72] Keen to ensure that no emotional wounds remained, a few months later Muhammad allocated a portion of the spoils of war taken at Khaybar to any participants in the march to Hudaybiyyah who were not present at Khaybar.

Leading by Example

The fact that Muhammad, seen by his followers as both a divinely appointed prophet and a political leader akin to a tribal chief, toiled alongside his comrades digging the massive trench during the aforementioned battle, testifies to his belief in leading by example.

This was not the first time that he had laboured alongside his followers. After arriving in Medina in 622 CE, he set about building the city's first bespoke mosque for collective prayer — made from mud bricks, palm trunks and fronds, with large stones as gate frames[73] — part of which would serve as his personal and family quarters. Ibn Hisham notes that Muhammad himself laboured in the construction, with the hope that this would "encourage Muslims to work".[74]

The exemplary nature of his leadership – that he strove always to show a willingness to do what he asked of others, however arduous or unpleasant, and that he believed the best way of teaching moral conduct was always to remain moral himself, is commented on in the Qur'an:

لَقَدْ كَانَ لَكُمْ فِي رَسُولِ اللَّهِ أُسْوَةٌ حَسَنَةٌ لِمَن كَانَ يَرْجُو اللَّهَ وَالْيَوْمَ الْآخِرَ وَذَكَرَ اللَّهَ كَثِيراً.

> Certainly, you have in Allah's Messenger an excellent example to follow for whoever puts their hope in Allah and the Last Day and remembers Allah a lot.[75]

Not only did he exert himself digging the trench alongside much younger men – he was then aged 56 – but he ate no more than anyone else and become so hungry after three days that he discretely tied a rock tightly to his stomach to ease the hunger pangs.[76] He tried to keep it covered, but at one point during strenuous exertion breaking a boulder, his comrades saw the bound stone. One of them felt so concerned that he went and told his wife to prepare a small meal for Muhammad. Upon learning that the wife had prepared only enough for him and maybe one or two others, the Prophet shocked her and her husband (who exclaimed: "To Allah we belong and to Him we return," the exclamation ordinarily made upon news of a death) by calling *all* the diggers to share the meal.[77] Islamic tradition records this event as a miracle: because Muhammad would not eat while others did not, everyone was sated and there was even some food left over.

As a prophet and communal leader, Muhammad was entitled to special treatment, such as eating better while campaigning with his men. Yet he ate only what his warriors ate and suffered privations — intense heat, hunger and thirst, exhaustion and discomfort — equally with them.[78] When he led a force of slightly over three hundred warriors to Badr in March 624, for example, they had only seventy camels between them. Three or four men therefore rode cramped on each camel.[79] Muhammad asked for no preferential treatment, even though no one would have begrudged him the right to ride alone, and he uncomfortably shared his camel with 'Ali ibn Abi Talib and Zayd ibn Harithah (some sources say Marthad ibn Abi Marthad al-Ghanawi).

Setting an example like this had a very positive effect. We know, for example, that when the Prophet set out for Tabuk in northern Arabia at the head of around 30,000 troops six years after Badr, it was intensely hot and the journey was long, arduous and hunger-inducing. The Prophet's willingness to suffer in the heat was noticed by his men, and even by stragglers and truants. 'Abdullah ibn Khaythama al-Salami had dallied in Medina after Muhammad had departed for Tabuk. One day, his two wives cooled their huts by spraying them with water and prepared food for him. Feeling ashamed that Muhammad was struggling northward in the heat, 'Abdullah exclaimed: "Praise be to God. The Messenger of God, already forgiven of all sins, did not delay despite the sun, the wind and the heat, and he carried his own weapons around his neck. But I am in the cool shade, with food and two beautiful women. This is not right. ... By God, I must go out and join the Messenger of God."[80] Despite his wives' objections, he knelt his camel, tightened its saddle, slung on his provisions, and immediately set off after Muhammad. When he finally caught up with the army, Muhammad was delighted and welcomed him without a hint of annoyance at his initial reluctance.

The last decade of Muhammad's life included almost constant armed struggle and thus the ever-present specter of death. Muhammad did not like fighting, and preferred to solve disputes through mediation and diplomacy, but recognised that coercion and warfare were sometimes inevitable or necessary, and that good could flow even from just and proportionate fighting. The Qur'an itself says:

كُتِبَ عَلَيْكُمُ الْقِتَالُ وَهُوَ كُرْهٌ لَّكُمْ وَعَسَى أَن تَكْرَهُواْ شَيْئاً وَهُوَ خَيْرٌ لَّكُمْ وَعَسَى أَن تُحِبُّواْ شَيْئاً وَهُوَ شَرٌّ لَّكُمْ وَاللّهُ يَعْلَمُ وَأَنتُمْ لاَ تَعْلَمُونَ

> Fighting is prescribed for you [believers] although it is something you hate, but perhaps you hate something that might be good, and love something that might be bad. Allah knows what you do not know.[81]

Again, Muhammad led by example, placing himself in the same danger and risk of death that he asked his warriors to face. Despite profound religious belief, he was human and sometimes deeply anxious. Al-Waqidi states that, at the Battle of Badr, when Muhammad saw the vastly stronger enemy force drawing nearer, he became "fearful" (فزِع, which could also mean "shocked") in the privacy of his hastily erected command hut. He raised his hands and implored God to fulfil his promises.[82] Ibn Hisham does not mention fear or shock in his own account, but notes that Abu Bakr, Muhammad's closest companion, took his hand and advised him to cease his fretful prayers, lest he convey anxiety to the God who had promised him success.[83] The event is also recorded in many ahadith, with Abu Bakr's calming gesture present in most, although again no shock or fear is mentioned.[84] This might be because, even if the very mortal Muhammad did feel anxious, he immediately steeled his nerve and soon thereafter powerfully exhorted his warriors to fight by advancing, not retreating, in the certainty that if anyone fell, he would enter Paradise.[85]

Ibn Hisham reveals that Muhammad's soldiers were so inspired by his exhortation that one, 'Umayr ibn al-Humam, flung down the dates he was eating, grabbed his sword and hurled himself upon the enemy. Another, 'Auf ibn Harith, threw off his heavy coat of mail and fought until he was killed. Muhammad then defiantly took a handful of pebbles and symbolically threw them at the enemy, ordering his own men forward. Victory came soon after.[86]

Muhammad's insistence that only determination and firmness in the face of fear are capable of bringing victory is found in many ahadith which quote him stating that "deserting the march" to a battle or "fleeing from the battlefield" are among the very worst human acts.[87] The Qur'an exhorts believers to be courageous and steadfast:

يَا أَيُّهَا الَّذِينَ آمَنُواْ إِذَا لَقِيتُمُ الَّذِينَ كَفَرُواْ زَحْفاً فَلاَ تُوَلُّوهُمُ الأَدْبَارَ.

وَمَن يُوَلِّهِمْ يَوْمَئِذٍ دُبُرَهُ إِلاَّ مُتَحَرِّفاً لِّقِتَالٍ أَوْ مُتَحَيِّزاً إِلَى فِئَةٍ فَقَدْ بَاء بِغَضَبٍ مِّنَ اللّهِ وَمَأْوَاهُ جَهَنَّمُ وَبِئْسَ الْمَصِيرُ.

O you who believe, when you encounter [in battle] those who disbelieve, do not turn your backs on them.

For whoever turns his back on them on that day, except that it be a tactical maneuver or to join another group, has indeed incurred Allah's wrath and his bode is Hell, a wretched destination.[88]

Courage is not fearlessness; rather, it is overcoming the natural human urge for self-preservation and ignoring peril in order to act selflessly on behalf of others. Not everyone can overcome the fear that grips them during battle, but Muhammad believed that his own example could strengthen the courage of the fearful.

During the Battle of Uhud he personally organised his warriors into the lines and groups he wanted, positioning them carefully where he thought they would prove most effective. He gave a rousing speech exhorting them to be steadfast and courageous. He then fought among his soldiers and exposed himself to such risks that he was in fact wounded by a projectile which struck his face and knocked him senseless for a few minutes. At one point, enemy troops were thronging to kill him and six devoted comrades made a human shield to project him. They all died defending him, with Abu Dujana using his own body to intercept arrows fired at him. He died with many arrows protruding from his body. The Prophet continued fighting, with other warriors defending him whilst shouting "my soul instead of yours".[89]

That does not mean that even the most rousing and courageous leadership will always prevent fear from overcoming people in battle. Humans are unpredictable and inconsistent. For example, at the Battle of Hunayn in 630 CE, which ended with a great and bountiful victory for Islam, there was a point when events swung against Muhammad. The enemy force surprised the Muslims while they were setting up their camp and showered them with arrows before rushing upon them on foot and horseback from hidden positions, forcing many to flee in fear and disorder, with horses and camels bumping into each other and cries and shouts of terror filling the air.

Here we see what Muhammad was made of. He did not panic. Standing high in the stirrups on the back of a white mule in the midst of the pandemonium, closely protected by ten of his most loyal companions with another hundred fighting bravely around them against far greater numbers, he waved his sword and shouted repeatedly to his troops to stop and gather around him. His cousin Abu Sufyan ibn al-Harith, who had only recently converted to Islam, steadied Muhammad's terrified mule, calming it while chaos swept around them.[90] Muhammad's courage and calls had the desired effect. The bulk of panicked Muslim troops regrouped and returned to the fight, soon securing for Muhammad a total victory.

The personal devotion that Muhammad was able to inspire was something that even Abu Sufyan ibn Harb — a close relative of Muhammad but also an antagonist who led several major military campaigns against him — had to acknowledge. In 625 CE two Muslims were captured, sold into slavery in Mecca, and sentenced to execution in reprisal for losses in the Battle of Badr.[91] Khubayb ibn 'Adi and Zayd ibn al-Dathinna faced their looming execution bravely, even after learning that they would die horrifically by painful crucifixion and stabbing with spears. They both rejected offers of release if they would renounce Islam and denounce Muhammad.

One after the other they were asked whether they wished Muhammad were in their place, with them safely back home, to which they replied that they did not wish it. They died horrifically yet without denouncing their leader. Al-Akhnas ibn Shariq later said that he had never seen a father as devoted to a son as Muhammad's companions were to him. Abu Sufyan ibn Harb, who eventually converted and became a great Muslim leader and military commander, himself said: "No, we have never seen the companions of any man who loves him more than Muhammad's companions love him."[92]

Common Touch

Muhammad undoubtedly had the common touch; the ability to relate and appeal to ordinary people from all walks of life, and this was central to his appeal as a leader. People wanted to follow him because of the rapport they felt with him. They knew he was different, of course. He was a prophet and a leader, with scrupulously righteous conduct, but he never adopted an air of superiority and seemed in many ways to be a normal man with ordinary interests who smiled and cried at, or liked and disliked, many of the same things as everyone else.

For example, he reportedly admired wrestling, and even as a man of advanced years, he enjoyed the thrill of what might seem a purely worldly activity. When he was around fifty he happened to come across Rukana ibn 'Abdu Yazid ibn Hashim ibn 'Abdul-Muttalib ibn 'Abdu Manaf, the Quraysh tribe's strongest man.[93] He could not pass up the opportunity to share Islam with Rukana, asking him why he had not yet accepted his religious invitation. Rukana replied that he might if he could be sure of the truth of Muhammad's message. Muhammad asked Rukana whether he would accept the message if Muhammad could throw him to the ground. Rukana said yes, only to find himself thrown by the much older man. He challenged Muhammad to try it again, which he did to the wrestler's amazement. Many Muslims today are less familiar with this story than they are of a hadith which has become popular and which reflects Muhamad's ability to use everyday things to communicate moral and spiritual truths: "The strong man is not one who wrestles well but the strong man is one who controls himself when he becomes angry."[94]

Muhammad also enjoyed horse and camel racing, and accordingly arranged public races and sometimes rewarded the winners from his own money.[95] Trained horses raced the six miles between Al-Hafiya and Al-Wada' while the untrained horses raced the one mile between Thaniyyat al-Wada and the Mosque of Banu Zuraiq. The Prophet later said: "I was among those who raced, and my horse jumped along with me over a wall."[96] A hadith richly captures the atmosphere at such races:

> Allah's Prophet ﷺ had a camel, 'Adba, which was almost impossible to surpass in a race. Then a Bedouin came riding his camel, which was younger than six years, and that camel beat it [i.e., 'Adba] in the race. The result was hard on the Muslims. The Prophet ﷺ noticed and stated the following [to console them]: "It is Allah's law that everything that goes up has to come down."[97]

The Prophet also believed that archery was both an enjoyable and rewarding pastime, and should be taught to boys, as he had himself learned it, and also practiced through life:

> Practice archery and practice riding. That you should practice archery is even more beloved to me than that you should ride. All idle pastimes that the Muslim engages in are pointless, except for his shooting of his bow, his training of his horse, and his playing with his wife, for they are from truth.[98]

He even taught that, if one had learned archery, and then grown tired of it, he had rejected or become ungrateful for what was in fact a blessing.[99]

Naturally, mastery of archery brought a tangible benefit. Arrow wounds killed and disabled more people in Arab battles than swords and spears. In preparation for fighting, Muhammad once exhorted: "Prepare to meet them with as much strength as you can muster. Beware, in archery is strength. Beware, in archery is strength. Beware, in archery is strength."[100] He added: "So let none of you forsake practicing with his arrows."[101]

It was because horse and camel racing and archery were highly beneficial skills for warriors, and therefore needed to be mastered during this era when campaigning occurred every year, that Muhammad made it permissible to gamble on these activities (with some restrictions on the knowledge of the outcome's certainty, and whether participants and non-participants could lay bets or benefit).

Games of chance and gambling on everything else had been banned, based on clear and unarguable Qur'anic revelation. Yet the skill and training involved in racing and archery, plus the enormous societal benefit of fostering excellence in these necessary martial activities, allowed Muhammad to offer something of an exemption. A hadith states: "Allah's Messenger ﷺ said: wagers are allowed only for racing camels or horses or shooting arrows."[102]

Muhammad intuitively knew that his best hope for building an effective leader-follower relationship with others was to create an egalitarian society in which everyone would benefit from the growing prosperity of his polity, and in which they all saw him among them and had easy access to him.

Rapport meant a lot to him. He greeted everyone he passed in the street, even any children who were playing[103], and was known to make time for anyone, including or perhaps especially the poor and powerless.

Once a woman who suffered from mental issues called out to him across the street, telling him that she needed something from him. He replied softly to her: "Mother, … tell me on which side of the street you would prefer me to speak with you so that I can do what is best for you." He then stood and listened to what troubled her.[104] Similarly, when a Bedouin once urinated in the mosque, infuriating many Muslims, Muhammad called out not to prevent or harm him. Instead, he asked for a jug of water and then went and washed where the man had urinated. He explained to his followers that he had been sent to make things easy for them, not difficult.[105] According to one hadith, he spoke calmly to the Bedouin, who recalled: "He [Muhammad] got up and came to me, and may my father and mother be ransomed for him, he neither rebuked nor reviled me, but only said: 'This mosque is not for urinating in. Rather it is built for the remembrance of Allah and prayer.'"[106]

Muhammad clearly had affection for children, and was often seen playing with them or carrying them on his shoulders. Once when addressing his followers from the pulpit, he noticed two of his infant grandchildren, Al-Hasan and Al-Husayn, waddling in unsteadily. He walked down, scooped them up, and carried them back up onto the pulpit.[107] He was especially fond of one granddaughter, Umamah, and once during the solemnity of communal prayers, of which he was the leader, enjoyed the fun of playing with her:

> The Messenger of Allah ﷺ led the people in prayer while she was on his shoulder. When he bowed he put her down and took her up when he got up. He kept on doing so until he finished his prayer.[108]

He even noticed that one toddler, a brother of Anas ibn Malik nicknamed Abu 'Umair, loved a pet bird. Every time he saw the boy Muhammad inquired after the bird.[109] These acts cemented in the minds of his followers their belief that Islam was for everyone, even the unimportant and most debased, and that their prophet cared about them and really did have the common touch.

Muhammad liked courtesy and good manners, but hated artifice, formality, and hierarchy, or to be treated with fawning deference. He did not like people to bow to him, kiss his feet or flatter him. After he emigrated to Medina he initially stayed in the house of Abu Ayyub, sleeping downstairs while Abu Ayyub and his wife slept above him. They found it terribly disrespectful to be above Muhammad, God's prophet, and asked him to swap places. He politely refused, instead telling them that he preferred it downstairs because it was easier for guests.[110]

Despite his companions sometimes suggesting he should dress more regally especially when delegations arrived, he refused,[111] preferring to wear the coarse clothing worn by the ordinary people. When he received gifts that were ostentatious or even just unnecessary, he was quick to give them away, usually to companions or the poor. He was so "ordinary" in the way he dressed and so humble in the way he carried himself among his companions that, when a Bedouin named Dimam ibn Tha'laba once came to Medina looking to ask the famous prophet some questions, he scanned the Muslims gathered in the mosque but was unable to distinguish which one was Muhammad.[112]

Perhaps most significantly, his community could see that he never enriched himself at their expense, but, instead, worked hard to raise everyone's living standard and to erase poverty. This he did by careful and judicious dispersal of both *sadaqah* (صدقة), alms given by believers for onward distribution, and *zakat* (زكاة). This was an obligatory charity tax collected by paid representatives of the polity for Muhammad to distribute to the poor, needy, stranded travelers and burdened debtors as well as to use for the inducement of alliances, the manumission of slaves, and — at a time when there was no standing army — the purchase of weapons and equipment for warfare.

Muhammad never appropriated anything for himself or his family, and on one occasion even made his little grandson, Al-Hasan, spit out one of the dates that had been given as charity. "Don't you know that we can't eat anything given [for the poor] as charity?"[113]

As a prophet and chieftain, he was formally entitled by Arabic custom to a substantial source of income: one-fifth (خُمْس, *khums*) of all income generated by campaigning.[114] This is less than the quarter that other Arab chiefs customarily took. The Qur'an is clear that this *khums* was not for Muhammad's enrichment, but was for him and his family to live on and also, and especially, to devote as he saw best to fighting poverty and inequality:

وَاعْلَمُوا أَنَّمَا غَنِمْتُم مِّن شَيْءٍ فَأَنَّ لِلَّهِ خُمُسَهُ وَلِلرَّسُولِ وَلِذِي الْقُرْبَىٰ وَالْيَتَامَىٰ وَالْمَسَاكِينِ وَابْنِ السَّبِيلِ إِن كُنتُمْ آمَنتُم بِاللَّهِ وَمَا أَنزَلْنَا عَلَىٰ عَبْدِنَا يَوْمَ الْفُرْقَانِ يَوْمَ الْتَقَى الْجَمْعَانِ وَاللَّهُ عَلَىٰ كُلِّ شَيْءٍ قَدِيرٌ

And know that whatever you take as gains of war, to Allah belongs one fifth, for the Messenger and his kinsfolk and for orphans, the poor, and the wayfarers. [Observe this] if you truly believe in Allah and what We sent down on our Servant on the day of judging; the day when the two forces met [at Badr]. Allah has power over everything.[115]

We know from the ahadith and the biographical sources, especially Ibn Hisham, Al-Waqidi and Ibn Sa'd, that Muhammad was scrupulously impartial in the way he allocated the other four-fifths of any bounty generated by battle, giving participants and approved absentees equal shares regardless of status or perceptions of strength or weakness. As he once explained, "I neither give to you, nor withhold from you, but I am merely a distributor and I allocate as I am obliged."[116] We also know that he never took more than his entitlement, and that — with the only exception being occasional one-off rewards to warriors for distinguished service or to induce loyalty from other tribes, which he paid from his own fifth of the *khums* — he steadfastly used the *khums* for the purposes mentioned in the Qur'an.[117] Sometimes from the *khums* he actually chose not to take his entitlement (i.e., the one-fifth of the one-fifth).[118]

He often used his own money for the community, rather than spending it on himself. We know, for example, that after the expulsion of the Banu Nadir tribe from Medina, which resulted in the seizure of many of their possessions as his sole right (the expulsion did not come through battle so were not regular spoils), Muhammad spent the money on horses and weapons for the army.[119]

He and his family also lived simply, for instance eating bread made from ground barley rather than refined white flour, and devoted the rest to social programs. Shortly before he died, he had so little money left that he used his own iron armour as security for a loan to buy barley for his family.[120] When he died, all he owned was that armour, his white mule, and a piece of land in Khaybar that he had received as his *khums* but which he did not pass on to his children because, he said, prophets should not die owning property. It was therefore given away as *sadaqah*.[121]

Strategic Vision

The fact that Muhammad eschewed the trappings of power and comfort, and saw his role as a servant, does not mean that he lacked ambition for his ever-burgeoning community. On the contrary, his strategic vision — his rare gift of being able to see the potential growth of the initially unpopular religious ideas he considered important as well as the social and political framework that he would need to create to sustain and protect those ideas — is a remarkable leadership quality. Able to bring the future close, he had a telescopic vision of Arabia and the world. He could see faraway things as though they were close, and he was able to make them sound so desirable and meaningful to others that they wanted to make the journey with him.

Even when he started his ministry and faced stiff opposition from Meccan traditionalists who accused him of bid'a (بدعة, innovation) for condemning the idolatry that lay at the heart of Mecca's role as a pilgrimage center, Muhammad possessed tremendous political intelligence and foresight. He turned the accusation back on the accusers, persuasively arguing that his way of understanding and serving God was neither an innovation nor a heresy, but that indeed, he was only trying to restore what *they* had over generations betrayed and damaged: the lost legacy of Abraham, Ishmael, and God's other beloved messengers. This put them on the back foot and attracted the young, the reform-minded, the pious and the suffering.

We have already seen above, in the way he exploited a short-term setback at Hudaybiyyah to create a long-term opportunity, how strategic and forward-looking he was. Even during brief moments of despondency, he never wavered in his total conviction that, with God's support, he could create a new confessionally inclusive monotheistic community in which "believers," even including some Jews and Christians if they were sufficiently pious and accepted his leadership, could flourish in God's service.[122] Regardless of tribe, status, or wealth, anyone could belong and everyone mattered. This was heady stuff, attracting and inspiring more and more people as the message spread.

That Muhammad envisaged such a community is indisputable. Shortly after emigrating to Medina in 622, he created what many Muslims now too grandly call the Constitution of Medina (دستور المدينة), a covenant or agreement between Muhammad and his own followers — then known as the Muhajirun (المهاجرون) and the Ansar (الأنصار); i.e., the believing "emigrants" who journeyed to Medina and the believing "helpers" already there — and the other tribes of Medina.[123] The text survives in Ibn Hisham's *Al-Sirah al-Nabiwiyyah* and Abu 'Ubayd al-Qasim ibn Sallam's *Kitab al-Amwal*.

Scholars disagree whether the various parties actually signed copies, whether there was a single agreement or several agreements later stitched together in records to look like a cohesive whole, or whether there were merely verbal agreements between leaders. Yet few scholars dispute the agreement's historicity.

Muhammad believed that his agreement would serve as the basis of a new religious polity that would transcend the old competitive tribal structure by binding the various Muslim, Jewish, and other Arab tribes or clans into "a single community [*umma*] to the exclusion of other people" ("انهم امة واحدة من دون الناس").[124]

Holding all these entities together as a community in terms of what we now call domestic and foreign policies, this agreement contained declarations of unity and equality, ethical expectations, and even a mutual defense pledge between people who had never previously been joined: monotheistic believers from different faith confessions and pagans. The agreement was not talking of any doctrinal or liturgical melding or hybridisation. It affirmed that "the Jews have their *din* [دين, religious ways] and the Muslims have their *din*"[125], but it also created an overarching framework for coexistence, tolerance, moral and behavioural standards, conflict resolution and mutual support. When one considers that Muhammad was recently a ridiculed and persecuted figure in Mecca and then a new arrival in Medina with fewer than 200 followers among many thousands of others citizens who still followed their own chiefs for a time, one can only conclude that his strategic vision was stupendously innovative, bold and forward-looking.

Muhammad understood that his vision was grandiose. He was not seeking only to reform either Mecca or Medina, to return them to a pure and pious monotheism, but to create a way for *all* humans to live. He would start first with the Arabs of the Hejaz, then spread the glad tidings and warnings to all people everywhere. As he said: "I have been sent to all humans, whereas the prophets before me were sent to their own people."[126]

This was indeed a far bolder vision than even Jesus possessed. Jesus claimed only to come for the lost sheep of Israel and he saw no possibility of, or value in, gaining any worldly power. Muhammad brought a message not only to Meccans and Medinans, and not only to the increasing number of Arabs in other tribes with whom he forged alliances, but to all humans. After all, the Qur'an said:

وَمَا أَرْسَلْنَاكَ إِلَّا رَحْمَةً لِلْعَالَمِينَ

We did not send you [Muhammad] except as a mercy for humanity.[127]

Through conviction, strength of character and charisma, Muhammad was able to convince increasing numbers of people to accept this bold religious-social-cultural-political global vision. During the early years in Medina progress was slow and stumbling, although Muhammad used his profound understanding of the very tribal system he eschewed to function as a sheikh himself, thereby growing his leadership beyond the limited role as a mediator that the Medinans may have originally foreseen for him. With intuitive and prodigious diplomatic skill, he negotiated an ever-enlarging network of alliances between his Islamic community (not Medina as such) and neighbouring towns and tribes. Like other Arab leaders, he initiated or accepted a number of shrewd and effective alliances through marriage.

The Jewish tribes remained religiously non-responsive and felt disinclined to see their participation in this community in the same terms that Muhammad did. Despite many Jewish individuals either embracing Islam or bonding in friendship with Muhammad and the Muslims, and with scattered Jewish villages and towns accepting his authority and living unmolested, the leadership of the three main Medinan Jewish tribes took their people into different types of rebellion. The result was that, after Muhammad had been in Medina five years, relatively few Jews still lived there and none did so in tribal units.

Jews nonetheless lived elsewhere in Arabia, as did Christians, and by 630 CE, when Muhammad's coalition army of 10,000 "opened" Mecca in a virtually bloodless liberation, an almost complete version of Muhammad's bold vision for a community existed throughout much of the Arabian Peninsula. Jewish and Christian minority communities lived without molestation in return for a poll tax that conversely exempted them from military service and the obligatory *zakat* charity tax. It is worth pondering the transformation of Muhammad's political fortunes: in 622, he and around seventy Muslims had emigrated from Mecca to Medina. Only eight years later Muhammad was able to lead 10,000 in the other direction. It was a remarkable *volte-face*.

We must resist the temptation to attribute this success to Muhammad possessing something akin to a modern understanding of what we would today call "strategy," especially if we mean political strategy or military strategy. That would simply be anachronistic.

Today we understand strategy to mean the setting of feasible, transforming, high-level and long term goals. These are the "ends" to which effort is concentrated based on carefully calculated "means", which are the people and resources available, and the artfully designed "ways", which are the sequential steps that need to be taken to apply the means in the optimal quantity at the right place at the right time.

Muhammad never provided any strategic framework like this to his activities. If he did, and applied ordinary judgment to it, he would have immediately recognised that his desired end state — the submission of all humans to the One God — was going to be unachievable in his lifetime with the means available to him.

That he sought such an end state is clear. The Qur'an calls itself "a reminder to humanity" (إِنْ هُوَ إِلَّا ذِكْرٌ لِّلْعَالَمِينَ) and, as seen above, states that Muhammad is a "mercy for humanity" (رَحْمَةً لِّلْعَالَمِينَ).[128] The Qur'an talks about the Last Day, "when humanity will stand before the Lord of the Worlds" (يَوْمَ يَقُومُ النَّاسُ لِرَبِّ الْعَالَمِينَ).[129] In 306 different verses, the Qur'an addresses all humans directly: "O, humanity, …" (يَا أَيُّهَا النَّاسُ).

It was natural and logical for Muhammad to want this end state. After all, ideologies are coherent belief systems based on *universal* values; that is, they rest upon a notion that the thing at their heart — which might be altruism, freedom, equality, security, or a combination of such things — is beneficial not only to some people, but to all people everywhere. Karl Marx did not believe that only some people would benefit from communism. He believed that everyone would. Democrats do not believe that democracy is good only for people in their country; they believe it would be good for all people everywhere. Likewise, Muhammad wanted every good thing for all humans everywhere. He believed that these things could only exist if people submitted to the One God. This meant, in his mind, that all people everywhere should submit to the One God.

The nature of profound religious belief is such that logical considerations about ends, means and ways are relatively unimportant, and certainly pale in consideration compared to the belief that God has limitless power and is capable of creating changes or delivering outcomes that non-religious strategists would see as impossible. Muhammad saw God in this fashion and believed that, as God's prophet, he could even pursue strategic goals that might seem ridiculous to others.

Ultimately, Muhammad believed that God had a masterplan, and that his own responsibility was to bring *that* to fruition. Indeed, he believed what the Qur'an asserted: that God was "the best of planners" (وَاللَّهُ خَيْرُ الْمَاكِرِينَ).[130] He therefore used to pray: "My Lord, help me and do not give help against me. Grant me victory, and do not grant victory over me. Plan on my behalf and do not plan against me. Guide me, and make this guidance easy for me."[131]

This does not mean that Muhammad did not himself plan. He certainly did. Nor does it mean that, in terms of each of the sequential steps to be taken in pursuit of his gloriously outsized goals, he did not consider the practicalities of ends, means and ways. He understood that actions created opportunities, and that to gain the most from these one needed to have plans and resources. He ordered a census of Muslims in Medina at one point, which is evidence that he was trying to work out precisely what human capital he had to play with.[132] He kept and regularly updated lists of his people so that he knew what strength he could apply to certain problems.[133] He kept himself abreast of his community's finances, even checking *zakat* accounts with the gatherers when they brought the payments to him.[134] At each stage of his polity's growth he carefully planned and proportionately resourced what he needed to do to reach the next stage. The early sources reveal many cases of him devising sequences of actions that would, step-by-step, deliver him what he wanted.

For example, during the crucial years 627 and 628 CE he faced rivals or enemies to the north of Medina and to the south. In the northeast his main concern was the powerful Ghatafan tribe, which had half-heartedly united once before with the Meccans in what became the Battle of the Trench in 627 CE. At that time the coalition fell apart due to lack of commitment, adverse weather, poor logistics and squabbles between the Ghatafan and the Quraysh (partly instigated by Muhammad's insertion of a "plant" within the coalition). North of Medina was also the fortified Jewish oasis-city of Khaybar, where members of Banu Nadir had settled after their expulsion from Medina in 625 by Muhammad for treason during the Battle of Uhud. They naturally remained hostile and zealously tried to induce or entice other Arab tribes to join with them against Muhammad. The Prophet had managed to minimise the likelihood or impact of such alliances by sending raids against those groups, often taking their livestock as a warning not to ally themselves with Islam's enemies. Yet the risk remained. And south of Medina was Mecca itself, which was still committed to the destruction of Muhammad's growing polity. For Muhammad the cleansing of Mecca of polytheistic worship was a key ambition. He aimed to return the Ka'ba to the One God.

We should not underestimate the danger of Muhammad's situation. In his enemies' minds, and according to the norms of Arabic tribal warfare[135], the only solution was his community's eradication. Describing his intention to destroy the Islamic polity, the Quraysh leader Abu Sufyan ibn Harb told Muhammad in a letter after the Battle of the Trench: "In the name of God, I swear by al-Lat and al-'Uzza [his pagan gods], surely I came to you with my allies and indeed, we vowed not to return until we had eliminated you."[136] At one point, Abu Sufyan even swore to abstain from sexual relations until he had attacked and defeated the Islamic polity.[137] It was not just military defeat he sought, but "extermination" also, as Muhammad acutely understood.[138]

Muhammad's grave concern was that a new coalition, possibly involving Mecca and Khaybar, would form against him, this time being larger than his forces could withstand. Moreover, if he took his entire force out of Medina to deal with Khaybar in the north, the Meccans might storm north and take the empty Medina from the south. He also knew that he could not lead an army south from Medina to Mecca while either or both of the foes to the north, the Ghatafan and the embittered Jews of Khaybar, could march upon the undefended Medina. Caught in the middle, he therefore had to orchestrate a set of moves that would remove these threats once and for all.[139]

The opportunity came when he led his unarmed pilgrim column towards Mecca to perform an 'Umrah in early 628 CE. He left Medina well-guarded, taking with him only 1,400 men. As noted above, the Quraysh halted the Muslim pilgrimage at Hudaybiyyah, just north of Mecca. Yet the Quraysh felt obliged to choose diplomacy instead of either letting the Muslims enter Mecca unimpeded, which would make them look weak, or fighting the pilgrims, which would damage their claim to be impartial custodians of the shrine who welcomed, accommodated and protected all pilgrims. Trying to appear resolute but without causing bloodshed, the Quraysh agreed to sign a treaty with Muhammad barring him from entering that year, but promising peace for ten years and the right to make a pilgrimage the following year. This, they correctly reasoned, would finally end Muslim raids on Meccan caravans. Importantly, the Treaty of Hudaybiyyah contained a seemingly innocuous clause allowing both sides to create alliances of their own without violating the ten years of peace guaranteed between them.

While the imposition of the treaty looked to Muhammad's companions and followers like a humiliation, he saw within it tremendous potential strategic benefits. It not only formally bestowed upon him equal status with Meccan leaders, but also gave him a free hand to make alliances with nomadic and other tribes, which he could entice one by one away from Meccan influence. Most importantly, it meant that he could march north against Khaybar and destroy it as a center of enmity with no threat of an attack from the south by the Meccans.

After returning to Medina he did just that; he immediately moved against Khaybar in a victorious siege, thus permanently removing his gravest threat in the north. Before Khaybar fell, it unsuccessfully appealed to the Ghatafan for assistance, promising them half its date crops as payment.[140] Muhammad deceived the Ghatafan into believing that their own town was under imminent threat, so they declined to join the fray. When Muhammad learned of Khaybar's offer to the Ghatafan, he imposed this percentage of produce as his required tribute. When the Jews of Fadak, a prosperous oasis town northeast of Khaybar, heard about this arrangement, they hastily made a treaty with Muhammad, promising him the same amount.[141]

With great emotional intelligence, Muhammad gave considerable spoils taken from Khaybar to those who had undertaken the Hudaybiyyah journey, regardless of whether they had actually fought at Khaybar.[142] It was his way of permanently laying to rest any disquiet that may have remained. He also promptly married Safiyya bint Huyayy ibn Akhtab,[143] the widowed daughter of the slain ruler of Khaybar (and leader of the Banu Nadir expelled from Medina), thus making him effectively the heir to Khaybar's political leadership.[144] His marriage to Safiyya as an act of inter-tribal diplomacy is reminiscent of his equally political marriage to Juwayriyya bint al-Harith, the daughter of the chief of the Banu al-Mustaliq, whom Muhammad married after the defeat of her tribe in 627 CE. Now as a kinsman by marriage, Muhammad was able to free from bondage all the Banu al-Mustaliq captives: one hundred families.[145] The Banu al-Mustaliq promptly joined the Islamic polity.

Muhammad also looked ahead strategically to how best to

bring the southern tribes into his ever growing polity. Recognising the high status that most tribes and groups accorded to the two most influential sedentary tribes, the Quraysh in Mecca and the Thaqıf in Ta'if, he reasoned that if he could win over those two tribes, he would also bring in the satellite tribal groups and the Quraysh's and the Thaqif's allies. That is precisely what he accomplished in 630. When he marched on Mecca, the Quraysh promptly entered Islam, followed shortly after by the Thaqif who saw the value in joining what had clearly become the only show in town. With few exceptions, all the satellite tribes punctually followed suit.

Thus, Muhammad's ability to see far ahead, to prioritise and sequence activities to create the causality and circumstances he desired, and to weigh costs and benefits so effectively, is testament to his creative, shrewd and pragmatic strategic statesmanship.

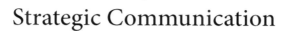

Strategic Communication

A great deal of this strategic success, which continued until Muhammad's death in 632 CE, and then of course after it under the direction of successors, can be attributed to his ability not only to explain God's will — he was seen by followers as humanity's final vessel for the outpouring of divine revelation — but also to his remarkable ability to communicate his own strategic vision and persuade people that it promised a desirable future.

Muslims see the words spoken by Muhammad as coming from two distinct sources: from God as revelation and from his own mind as inspiration. Whichever way readers of this book choose to see his spoken words, recorded in both the Qur'an and the ahadith, we can only conclude that almost no other human has ever spoken with influence as widespread and enduring.

Even non-Muslims who reject the view that God himself composed the Qur'anic words that Muhammad spoke cannot deny that the Qur'an is the second most widely read book in the world (surpassed in readership only by the Christian Bible), that millions of people have memorised it word-for-word (unlike the Bible) and almost two billion live according to its words.

Muhammad's "other" words (meaning those not counted as God's own words) are only slightly less known by Muslims. Although not considered sacred — that is, as scripture — the recorded sayings of Muhammad are the basis of the daily practice of the theology expounded by the Qur'an. It is reasonable to conclude, therefore, that Muhammad's actual spoken words are among the most known and followed words in human history.

Augmenting the Qur'anic message seamlessly and consistently in style and imagery, Muhammad used a rich palette of repeatedly uttered and easily learned and remembered parables, similes and metaphors to communicate his vast multi-faceted religious-social-cultural-political vision through a surprisingly small set of key messages.[146] These constantly communicated messages included the oneness of God and the obligation to please God through devotion and scrupulously moral conduct, through upholding societal cohesion, through using generosity to combat poverty, through being unfailingly good to other humans with whom coexistence is possible, and through the courageous and resolute fighting of those who choose aggression or reject coexistence.

Like Jesus, Muhammad could paint pictures with words. We thus learn from Muhammad that remembering God throughout the day is — as he encouragingly told a Bedouin from the dryness of the desert — like "always keeping your tongue moist".[147] We learn that a leader is not only a "shepherd," as noted above, but also a "shield for his people" who will always benefit from that protection.[148] We learn that someone who severs the "ties of the womb" (that is, family relations) will be judged for doing so.[149] Words of backbiting or personal unkindness are so bitter they would even "change the sea if they were mixed with it."[150] "Paradise," he said, "is beneath the feet of mothers."[151] It is also beneath the "shadow of swords".[152]

In single sentences he could convey profound truths. He once told the Ansar, after news reached him that tribute had arrived from Bahrayn: "I am not so much afraid of your poverty as of your wealth."[153] Similarly, emphasising his expectation that women be treated fairly and kindly, he cleverly made his point like this:

> A man came to Allah's Messenger ﷺ and said, "O Allah's Messenger ﷺ, who is most entitled to be treated the best by me?" The Prophet ﷺ replied, "Your moth-

er." The man asked, "Who is next?" The Prophet said, "Your mother." The man asked again, "Then who is next?" The Prophet ﷺ said, "Your mother." The man persisted, asking for the fourth time, "Who is next?" The Prophet ﷺ said, "Your father."[154]

Muhammad certainly understood the influence that the spoken word can have. In one hadith he commented on the power and eloquence of speech. After hearing two visitors from the east, he remarked: "Some eloquent speech has the influence of magic."[155] Although perhaps he meant it differently to the way we would use words like this now, he might well have been describing himself by saying that some speech is magical.

He used short, sincere and well-reasoned argumentation, considering himself blessed that he had received from God the gift of being able to speak concisely with the meaning nonetheless remaining comprehensive.[156] With the appearance of both sincerity and certainty that made him easy to believe and trust, he was a marvelous speaker with great presence and a transformational effect. In small speeches on large ideas about the establishment and growth of a just and egalitarian society in which everyone could benefit, he persuaded them that there was only one viable vision for Arabia and the world: the one that he compellingly proclaimed.

Muhammad's decision to establish a *khutba* (خطبة, sermon) every Friday was doubtless primarily to teach and disseminate the Qur'an, but it also gave him a powerful forum for reaching his followers directly with his grand agenda.[157] On Fridays he gave short, clear and hard-hitting sermons that were simultaneously religious, social, cultural, and political in nature. In his mind, his new reform movement was holistic, encompassing all these factors with no clear demarcation between any of them. By assembling snippets from ahadith we can see, within these sermons, the bigger picture repeatedly being stressed in order that everyone understood what God and Muhammad were trying to achieve, how people fitted into that plan as individuals and as a community, and what was required of them. This created a common understanding of the large ideas; the things that brought meaning and coherence to people who often felt unable to make sense of the chaotic and confusing society they were born into.

Yet we also find in the sermons enormous practicality, such as warnings about the likelihood of certain future activities[158] and guidance on how to create fair and transparent agreements and contracts with others, how to cope with famine or ask God for rain, how to deal militarily with a threat ("Prepare to meet them with as much strength as you can manage"[159]), and even how to behave properly during war, avoiding such horrors as cruelty and mutilation.[160]

Ahadith tell us that at least some of Muhammad's Friday sermons were written down[161], presumably for posterity but also so that those people who could read — which was only a very small minority even within the cities — could hear Muhammad's words verbatim. Presumably, written copies were also sent to other Islamic centers and communities in Arabia so they also could benefit. We know, for instance, that Muhammad himself ordered his first sermon in Mecca after its liberation to be written out for Abu Shah, a man from Yemen, so that he could take it back with him.[162]

Undertaking what today we call "strategic communication," he constantly articulated, repeated and reinforced his strategic vision to his burgeoning community, and he made sure that, as Islam spread and new mosques opened, the prayer leaders he appointed did the same. Knowing that other preachers would fail to persuade if they were seen as impious or unknowledgeable, he ensured that he sent out scrupulously moral men who were masters of the Qur'an and understood his vision. Their goal was the same as his: to help Muslims make sense of the complex, ambiguous and often difficult world around them, the challenges they collectively faced, and how they would, with God's mercy and strength, face them together.

To ensure that he and the assigned preachers had the widest possible audience at the sermons and attached prayers — which he believed provided profound spiritual benefits and were not merely for the conveyance of information — he forbade regular commercial activities for that time on Fridays in accordance with a qur'anic instruction:

يَا أَيُّهَا الَّذِينَ آمَنُوا إِذَا نُودِي لِلصَّلَاةِ مِن يَوْمِ الْجُمُعَةِ فَاسْعَوْا إِلَى ذِكْرِ اللَّهِ وَذَرُوا الْبَيْعَ ذَلِكُمْ خَيْرٌ لَكُمْ إِن كُنتُمْ تَعْلَمُونَ

فَإِذَا قُضِيَتِ الصَّلَاةُ فَانتَشِرُوا فِي الْأَرْضِ وَابْتَغُوا مِن فَضْلِ اللَّهِ وَاذْكُرُوا اللَّهَ كَثِيراً لَعَلَّكُمْ تُفْلِحُونَ

> O you who believe: on Friday when the call for prayer is made, then hasten to remember Allah and leave off all business. This would be better for you if only you knew it. Then when the prayer has finished, disperse within the land and [again] seek from the bounty of Allah, and remember Allah often that you will succeed.[163]

Just as an aside, Muhammad also used both the daily and Friday communal prayers as a means of tightening community cohesion. Everyone was to be present, they were to assemble in tight rows (ideal preparation for teaching the discipline needed during combat[164]), and they were to stand shoulder to shoulder, brothers together and sisters together.

The mosque layout and the ritual and liturgy within were all designed to aid the communication of a profound truth: that in this new religious community everyone had equal value in God's eyes, with no-one allocated status or privilege except that bestowed by their *taqwa* (تقوى); their fear of God, or piety. The front row was never allocated to whomever believed they mattered most in terms of tribal affiliation, status, wealth or ethnicity. Islam was a community of equals. Whoever loved God and his

Prophet enough to turn up early would pray at the front. With this in mind, and wanting the sermons heard by as many people as possible, Muhammad revealed a spiritual insight that he recognised would reach even the simpler people:

> The Prophet ﷺ said, "Every Friday the angels position themselves at the gates of the mosque to write the names of the people one by one [i.e. according to the time of their arrival for the Friday prayer] and when the imam sits [at the pulpit ready to speak] they fold up their scrolls and get ready to listen to the sermon."[165]

Muhammad surely never knew that Aristotle had once identified within effective rhetoric three interrelated components: *ethos* (the establishment of a message's credibility through trust in the speaker), *pathos* (the appeal to the audience's emotions in order to create empathy and connection) and *logos* (the appeal to rationality through logic and proof in order to build belief). We have no evidence that Muhammad ever theorised or formularised what he did as a speaker. Yet in his own untaught, intuitive and natural fashion, without artifice or any consciously copied habits, he was a masterful speaker who instinctively included all three of Aristotle's components.

He recognised that the way he spoke was as important as the content he wished to convey. When speaking one-on-one he devoted so much attention to any companion that the person felt that he or she was of utmost importance. He never spoke over people, or interjected if they were dragging on or he wished to make a point, but, rather, he waited.

Both in conversation and especially while speaking to crowds in the mosque or before battle, he spoke with deliberation, choosing words for simplicity, clarity and effect. Ibn Sa'd said that "he did not speak quickly and haphazardly," but with pauses allowing listeners to keep up and later recall.[166] He spoke slowly enough that even simple and uneducated people could follow.[167] He kept his speeches short, even religious sermons, so that they would neither bore nor exhaust the concentration span of listeners.[168] He once explained that any leader he appointed should prevent his speech or prayers dragging on — which is "off-putting" — because among audiences are "the sick, the weak and those with needs".[169]

He knew to appeal to both the mind and the emotions, and sometimes was so successful with the latter that he moved his audience to tears. 'Irbad ibn Sariyah once recalled: "One day, the Messenger of Allah ﷺ stood up among us and delivered a deeply moving speech that melted our hearts and caused our eyes to overflow with tears."[170]

He understood the value of reinforcing his key themes, using repetition to place stress on important points. Anas ibn Malik recalled that, whenever the Prophet wanted a message clearly understood, whether it was in the mosque or on the battlefield, "he used to repeat it thrice, so that the people could understand it properly."[171] One hadith demonstrates that this was not only for grand pronouncements, but also for very intimate occasions when he wanted to stress a point:

> A woman of the Ansar came to the Prophet ﷺ in the company of her children, and the Prophet ﷺ said to her, "By Him who holds my soul in His hand, you are the most beloved people to me!" And he repeated the statement three times.[172]

Frequently in speeches to large audiences, such as when delivering a sermon in the mosque or exhorting courage before battle, Muhammad masterfully used what today is called "call-and-response," a verbal interaction between a speaker and an audience which draws them together in a close and powerful fashion. It involves the speaker "calling" to the audience, ordinarily with questions likely to evoke an emotional verbal "response," a called reply from the audience. It is such an effective tool for closing the gap between speaker and audience that it is now ubiquitous at political rallies and rock concerts.

During his famous "Farewell Sermon" in 631 CE, which is an oratorical masterpiece, he climbed a small hill in front of around 100,000 adoring pilgrims, and cried out to them:[173]

"What day is it today?"

In unison they called back, "The day of sacrifice!"

He repeated it again twice, before calling out, "What city is this?"

In unison they called back, "The sacred city [i.e., Mecca]!"

He repeated the question again twice, before calling out, "What month is this?"

In unison they called back, "The sacred month!"

"No doubt," he told them, "and Allah has made your blood, your possessions and your honour sacred among each other like the day is sacred, the month is sacred and the city is sacred."

The Prophet then delivered his sermon, stripping the complexities of the Islamic message to its basics. He talked of the need to keep faith strong through prayer and remembrance of God, the rule of law, communal solidarity, and the importance of strict morality. These motifs had been central to his message for the previous twenty years. Now he once again reiterated them with certainty and clarity, appealing to both the rationality and emotions of his audience. To close, he stretched his hands to the sky and repeatedly cried aloud, "O people, haven't I conveyed Allah's message to you?" to which they shouted back each time: "Yes!"[174]

Muhammad also understood that an audience might be thoroughly gripped by a person's speech and convinced by its key assertions, but if people left without understanding what they were supposed to do with the ideas, the presentation would have been anticlimactic. Thus, to ensure that actions followed words, he placed effective calls for action into his speeches, ordinarily near or at the end of sermons or speeches. Here he told his audience what role they could play after they left. Sometimes he gave them concrete issues to deal with, and other times he created a moral imperative for action without specifying the exact requirement. In both cases, the intention was to get the audience to engage with the goals that were highlighted.

Perhaps aware that he might never again address such a crowd, he closed his Farewell Sermon with a very solemn call to action, this time initially with an instruction to refrain from doing something: "You shall meet your Lord and He will ask you about your deeds. Beware! Don't go astray after me by taking the lives of one another." He then finished with a positive action; the thing that they *should* now do: "Lo! It is incumbent upon those who are present today to share this [speech] with those who are absent for perhaps they might comprehend it better than some of you here."[175]

It would be easy to believe that Muhammad's great advantage in strategic communication was that when he conveyed new Qur'anic revelations — that is, when new verses came through him — his followers did not hear them as a man's words, but as God's words. The messages' ability to demand obedience and to convey truth was therefore highly magnified.

That was precisely how many people around Muhammad understood the revelations. Yet this reality camouflages an important truth: that at various times Muhammad received no divine revelation for considerable periods — after the first verses came, he may have received no more divine inspiration for almost three years — but in the meantime he nonetheless continued to teach, preach, guide and lead through his own gift of oratory.

In the interval between Qur'anic revelations Muhammad spoke from his own intuition and intellect, always stressing the common good over individual needs, to rouse the reluctant and inspire the insipid. During the earliest period when revelation came only sporadically, and was rather esoteric and abstract, Muhammad was able with his own almost hypnotic ability with words to transform people, mostly the young who are always drawn to the new and the bold. This ability helped him to create the fiercely loyal and dedicated nucleus of what would, after the emigration to Medina, quickly expand into an equally committed community.

He was so persuasive in speech that the Quraysh tribal leaders in Mecca, who resented his growing influence and what they considered insults to their own practices and the enticement of their young people, debated whether he was a soothsayer, shaman, sorcerer, demoniac or poet.[176] After debating each possibility, they concluded: "The nearest thing to the truth is that he is a sorcerer, who has bought a message by which he separates a man from his father, or from his brother, or from his wife, or from his family."[177]

At one point 'Utba ibn Rabi'a, one of the Quraysh tribal elders, sat with Muhammad and tried gently to reason with him, even offering him wealth, leadership and the provision of doctors to cure what he thought might be Muhammad's possession by a spirit. Muhammad listened patiently and respectfully, never interrupting, before reciting to him a Qur'anic message of hope and warning. 'Utba listened attentively and watched in fascination as Muhammad prayed and then again respectfully spoke with him. 'Utba then returned to his own circle, who noticed that his expression was unusual and asked what had happened. He explained that he had sat with Muhammad and had "never heard words spoken like this before, which were not poetry, spells or witchcraft." "Take my advice," 'Utba warned his peers, "and leave this man alone. For by God his words will be blazed abroad." They were appalled, telling him: "He has bewitched you with his tongue."[178]

The Qur'an contains echoes of these criticisms, including their statement:

فَقَالَ إِنْ هَذَا إِلَّا سِحْرٌ يُؤْثَرُ

إِنْ هَذَا إِلَّا قَوْلُ الْبَشَرِ

This is nothing but sorcery, derived of old. It is nothing but the word of a man.[179]

The Qur'an also offered correction:

وَمَا عَلَّمْنَاهُ الشِّعْرَ وَمَا يَنبَغِي لَهُ إِنْ هُوَ إِلَّا ذِكْرٌ وَقُرْآنٌ مُّبِينٌ

We have not taught him [Muhammad] poetry; it is not fitting for him. This is but a reminder and a clear Qur'anic recitation.[180]

We know that the power of his oratory was so moving that few could resist its ability to persuade. After the Battle of Hunayn, he apportioned the spoils, giving the largest share to Abu Sufyan ibn Harb, his former chief antagonist and a recent convert to Islam, and to other newly converted Meccans. He wisely did so to ensure their loyalty, which at that stage was still highly fragile. It nonetheless upset the Ansar, who felt that they had struggled for years on behalf of the Prophet, and were now being overlooked. Some suspected that, now that Muhammad had liberated Mecca, his hometown, he would live there again and not return to Medina, their city, even though they had given him refuge and ceaseless support. Was this unequal apportionment of spoils the result of favouritism? They said among themselves, and to their leaders: "If this decision is from Allah we will be patient, but if it is from Allah's Messenger we will ask for an explanation."[181] After all, this was the open environment of dialogue that Muhammad had fostered. Muhammad let people speak their minds regarding any decisions that had come from his own reasoning and not from revelation. Back when he had arrived in Medina eight years earlier, he had told people from the Ansar:

"I am a human, so when I command you about a thing pertaining to religion you should do it, and when I command you about a thing out of my personal opinion, keep in mind that I am [just] a human."[182]

The earliest biographical sources relate the entire remarkable exchange between the Ansar and the Prophet over the booty taken at Hunayn. Their accounts reveal Muhammad's political acumen and mastery of language and rhetorical persuasion. When he heard of the Ansar's dissatisfaction at being denied spoils of war, he asked to speak to Sa'd ibn Ubadah, the Ansar leader.[183] Sa'd reaffirmed the Ansar view that, if the decision came from God, they would be patient, but if it was Muhammad's decision, they wanted an explanation. Muhammad asked where Sa'd stood on the issue, to which he replied: "O Messenger of Allah, what am I except one of them?"

Muhammad then asked Sa'd to gather the disaffected, wanting to address them all rather than just Sa'd and other leaders. He knew it was important that everyone felt both included and valued. He then conveyed empathy, advising them that, yes, he understood that they were angry.[184] This was an important way of making them feel heard and appreciated. Then he appealed to their understanding, highlighting that spiritual benefits outweighed material gain:

> I came to you [in Medina] in your ignorance, and has not Allah guided you? I came to you in your poverty, and has not Allah already enriched you? In enmity, and has not Allah reconciled you?

They replied: "It is very true; Allah and His Messenger have been kind and gracious to us." He then asked why they would not speak further to support their case, to which they replied, "But what more can we say?" Muhammad then cleverly spoke on their behalf, putting himself in their place and emphasising their own kindness to him, thereby restoring to them a sense of honour and the certainty that he deeply appreciated them:

> By Allah, if you wanted you could have told me, and you would have been truthful, that you came to us discredited [O Muhamad], but we gave you our trust. You came alone, and we supported you. You were an outcast and we gave you asylum. You were distressed and we comforted you.

After this reaffirmation of the huge debt of gratitude he owed them, he advised them not to be so concerned about the affairs of the world, having become reconciled to God. Then, appealing to their emotions, he asked them to reflect on one key question:

> Are you not content that the people [of Mecca] will return only with cattle and camels, while you will return with the Messenger of Allah [to Medina]? By Him whose hand holds my soul, if it were not by circumstance, I would be an Ansar myself. If the people of Mecca went to a valley, and the Ansar to another valley, I would choose your valley to go to.[185]

He then told them not to feel discouraged; that whenever the riches of Bahrayn came to him, he would give it to them, and not to the Meccans. In the meantime, they should be patient, knowing that he would return to their city, not to Mecca, and that they would be given treasure in heaven, including bowls more numerous than the stars. He then stretched his hands to the sky and cried aloud: "O Allah, bless the Ansar, the children of the Ansar and the grandchildren of the Ansar."[186]

Hearing this, the Ansar were both satisfied and profoundly moved, weeping so much that their beards were wet and they sobbed loudly: "We are satisfied, O Messenger of God, with how you have benefitted us."[187] The matter was resolved, and they dispersed, with neither side holding the slightest grudge. It was an oratorical masterpiece, but only one of many recorded in the sources.

Military Leadership

As well as strong political intuition and ability and a gift for communication, Muhammad had what he himself called a sound grasp of military "judgment, strategy and tactics" (الـرَّأْيُ وَالْحَـرْبُ وَالْمَكِـيـدَةُ).[188] It is hard to argue against this, given that during only a decade, from 622 to 632 CE, he quickly transformed from an inexperienced and unsure military leader to a highly successful, routinely successful, and battle hardened military commander capable of skilfully handling armies with thousands of warriors.

The tribal nature of Arabian society tended to work against the establishment of any large-scale warfighting capability. Tribes and clans essentially lived with the assumption that a state of war existed between one's own tribe and all others unless a treaty or agreement with another tribe existed.[189] Tribes did frequently unite on an ad-hoc basis to deal with particular issues, but when military in nature these coalitions were seldom long-lasting and never permanent arrangements, partly due to decentralised leadership caused by sheikhs or leaders from each tribe or clan retaining authority over their own people. Sometimes coalitions would dissolve when one or more of the tribal or clan chiefs felt slighted by another chief or believed that he and his people had gained an acceptable amount of booty or prestige, even if the original aim of the coalition remained unfulfilled.

Recognising this, and wanting a more effective and reliable means of gaining security for his rapidly expanding *umma*, and knowing that only a cohesive and capable force under centralised command (his own) could act as the desired agent of change, Muhammad set about transforming tribal militias into what became, under his successors, a regular standing army.

Certainly by the time of the Battle of Khaybar in 628, Muhammad had largely created the army he knew he would need to achieve his strategic goals. It was not yet composed only of people whom today we would call professionals; that is, by full-time soldiers paid by the state to perform only that role. It was technically still a militia, a citizen army raised from the civil population to fight certain battles or undertake certain tasks. Yet the warriors were really doing little else. With a steady stream of smaller raids in between the bigger battles, the same people were constantly engaged in military affairs, becoming increasingly disciplined, experienced and expert. They were no longer seen as being Medinans or tribal members, but as a Muslim army — Arabia's first ever non-tribal army — and Muhammad alone was clearly its general. When this force fell upon the town of Khaybar early one morning, the panicked citizens cried out: "Muhammad and the army!" (محمد والخميس).[190]

Muhammad disliked war and sought other ways to solve disputes. He understood that war would only be moral if fought for just reasons.[191] This ordinarily meant that the *cause* of war was self-defence, pre-emption against enemies who were marshalling forces against the Islamic polity, security of Arabia's borders from greater external powers which might smother the Islamic polity in its infancy, and shows of offensive strength designed to coerce (with minimal or no bloodshed) other tribes into accepting his political leadership.

Even Muhammad's pre-emptive operations were ultimately self-defensive. For example, shortly after the occupation of Mecca, Muhammad felt compelled to initiate a vast offensive operation in the direction of Hunayn to meet a large coalition force of the Hawazin and Thaqif tribes, which his spies discovered was preparing to attack Mecca.[192] The Battle of Hunayn thus involved Muhammad marching out offensively to strike before being struck.

He also understood that even offensive operations should never involve the deliberate targeting or careless harming of the innocent, by which he meant women, children, priests and other religious figures, the aged, the infirm, agricultural and horticultural workers, as well as even the enemy's property and means of production.[193] These rules were innovative and strictly enforced.

Yet Muhammad understood that, if war did occur, he had to conduct it with vigour, focus and assertiveness. Because defensive actions seldom brought decisive results, he insisted that all military operations must be directed offensively whenever possible in order to gain, retain and exploit both freedom of action and initiative. By doing so, the opponents would be forced always to react to Muslim actions, rather than be able to conduct their own.

Resolute offensive action would also — as the Qur'an says — "create fear in the enemies of Allah and your enemy" (تُرْهِبُونَ بِهِ عَدْوَّ اللَّهِ وَعَدُوَّكُمْ)[194] and firmly deter other enemies who might want to follow their actions:

فَإِمَّا تَثْقَفَنَّهُمْ فِي الْحَرْبِ فَشَرِّدْ بِهِم مَّنْ خَلْفَهُمْ لَعَلَّهُمْ يَذَّكَّرُونَ

> If you meet them in combat, deal with them [resolutely] to deter those behind them, so that they may take heed.[195]

Muhammad correctly understood that frightening an enemy into deciding not to fight or behave threateningly or recklessly was an ideal way of preventing bloodshed on both sides. This is what U.S. President Theodore Roosevelt famously described 1,300 years later as the basis of statesmanship: "Speak softly and carry a big stick". Muhammad felt satisfied that, through resolute offensive actions, many of them being intended only as casualty-light demonstrations of strength, any potential enemies knew better than to cause mischief. He listed his ability "to strike awe [into enemies] from as far away as a month of journeying" as one of his unique attributes.[196]

Muhammad also recognised that carefully designed and sufficiently resourced security measures must be undertaken to permit the army's or detachment's freedom of offensive action whilst protecting his city and citizens by identifying and minimising all vulnerabilities to hostile attacks. Some of the leaders he left behind to protect the city, even his beloved 'Ali ibn Abi Talib, grumbled that they would much prefer to be away with him on campaign, rather than do what they considered nothing more than "looking after the women and children".[197] Little did they appreciate the importance of this solemn responsibility.

Muhammad worked tirelessly to maintain the morale of his troops, who usually had to forage for food and endure intense heat and hardship. He did this through constant engagement and frequent and focused praise and encouragement. With marvellous oratory, he repeatedly emphasised the nobility and necessity of the cause, publicly highlighted the valour of individuals, rewarded excellence, and gave successful people increasingly important responsibilities. In combat he made rousing supplications with the troops, such as: "There is no God but Allah, the One who confers upon His armies the honour of victory and helps His servants to rout the clans; nothing matters beyond that."[198] This was a powerful morale booster. With God supporting them, how could they doubt or fear or lose?

The Qur'an itself praised those who chose to serve, recognising them as being superior to those who evaded service as well as worthy of every material and spiritual reward.[199] Naturally there were some shirkers, described by the Qur'an as being sick of heart, unwilling to be inconvenienced by long journeys or heat, keen to stay home with their wives, reluctant to contribute financially despite their wealth, and even cowardly and fearful of defeat.[200]

Except for these people, who were actually few in number and later forgiven after being singled out for short-term shunning, Muhammad had no problem getting volunteers to serve.

The ahadith speak of plentiful volunteers whose names were inscribed in special military registers.²⁰¹ They also show that sometimes so many people volunteered that their names surpassed the ability to be listed in the registration books.²⁰²

At the heart of Muhammad's military leadership was the concept of unity. Even when he despatched a detachment of troops, but was unable to go himself, he appointed only one leader. He did so even if the detachment was composed of members of different tribes, clans or peoples. They would all obey that leader, as equals beneath him, even if they came from tribes of differing status or reputation, and regardless of which group the leader himself came from. Division or disobedience based on tribalism was unacceptable:

> The Messenger of Allah ﷺ said: "Whoever fights blindly for a cause which encourages tribalism or getting angry because of tribalism, then he has died in ignorance.²⁰³

No longer giving loyalty based on tribes, the warriors sent on missions were now "believers" and "brothers" united in obedience of a single leader. We see a reference to this concept in Muhammad's despatch to Nakhla of 'Abdullah ibn Jahsh as head of a detachment in January 624 CE. Al-Waqidi records that 'Abullah was called the "leader of the believers" (أمـير المؤمنـين) during that raid.²⁰⁴ We should not read too much into this phrase. It was not a formal rank or title, deserving of capital letters, as it became when chosen by Muhammad's political successors, but it indicative of the fact that the raids were led by people given responsibility for a cohesive and unified band of men defined not by tribe, but by belief.

Muhammad's strict insistence on unity of command can be seen clearly in the case of the raid on Dhat al-Salasil, which was ten days' journey north of Medina. He sent 'Amr ibn al-'As with a detachment of troops, hoping that 'Amr could drum up local support for a forthcoming expedition to Syria. Once in the enemy area 'Amr became afraid and sent to Muhammad for reinforcements. Muhammad despatched Abu 'Ubaydah ibn al-Jarrah with extra troops and a very clear instruction: "You two must not disagree."[205] When Abu 'Ubaydah reached 'Amr's position, the latter insisted that he remained in charge. Abu 'Ubaydah refused to be drawn into a dispute, telling 'Amr that the Prophet had insisted that they must not quarrel over command. He humbly submitted to 'Amr, saying: "Even if you disobey me, I will obey you." 'Amr gloated, saying: "Then I am your commander, and you are only my reinforcement." Complying with the Prophet was more important than succumbing to ego, so Abu 'Ubaydah merely replied: "Have it your way".[206]

It is also worth noting that, whenever Muhammad sent out a raid, he would personally meet with its leader to pray for the group's safety, to explain the mission's purpose, and to convey his trust in him. This must have been highly empowering. We also know that he would explain the moral behaviour he expected (for example, no harm to women, children and the aged, and no mutilation) and would also explain to him the need "to be good" to the people under his authority.[207]

Not wanting inter-tribal squabbles or doubts about authority to erupt if an appointed leader died in battle, Muhammad made clear before sending any force on a campaign that was likely to result in casualties who the officially appointed second-in-command was. In some cases he even named the third-in-command in case the first two fell. We see this most clearly before the Battle of Mu'tah, when Muhammad appointed his beloved adopted son Zayd ibn Harithah as commander, but "if he is martyred, then Ja'far [ibn Abi Talib] should take over, and if he is also martyred then 'Abdullah ibn Rawaha should take over."[208] As it happened, all three died in the battle, prompting Khalid al-Walid to assume authority on his own initiative. Possessing tremendous presence and charisma, and a long record of success as a warrior, the army accepted his command.

Fighting on raids and in battles involved solemn responsibilities not only for the leaders, but also for the warriors. Muhammad was clear that the new Islamic army he was creating would contain no disobedience, no pursuit of personal gain or reputation (often attained in Arab culture through ostentatious displays of reckless valour at the expense of the common good), and no misconduct whatsoever. As he said:

> Warfare involves two kinds [of warrior]: The one who fights for Allah's favour, obeys his leader, supports the mission with the property he values, treats his comrades gently and commits no misconduct [فساد, fasad] will gain reward while he is asleep and awake. Yet the one who fights for self-centered or arrogant reasons, who disobeys the leader or commits any misconduct in the land will miss out on reward with anything worthwhile.[209]

Fasad, often translated clumsily and innocuously as "mischief" or "corruption", actually denotes serious acts of unlawful killing, violence, immorality or insurrection. In the Qur'an it is listed as a major sin alongside murder.[210] In terms of warrior conduct, it meant killing the innocent or violating their rights, showing no mercy when it should be granted, torture, mutilation, stealing from the booty, or acting in ways that destroyed cohesion and comradeship.

Clearly Muhammad could not be calling other tribes and peoples to serve God and live according to a strict moral code if his army's actions represented a different set of values; even those ordinarily seen in Arab armies at that time. His army must be different.

That does not mean that Muhammad saw the use of force as lacking art or cunning. On the contrary, central to his military leadership was his desire to minimise danger and casualties by craftily outsmarting his enemies. He possessed an uncanny feel for what today we call ruses of war.

The Qur'an itself mentions such ruses including, for example, feigned retreats.²¹¹ Likewise, a hadith quotes Muhammad saying: "War is deceit" ("الْحَرْبُ خُدْعَةٌ"). The hadith is certainly authentic and considered reliable. It can be found in five of the six major Sunni hadith collections: *Sahih al-Bukhari*²¹², *Sahih Muslim*²¹³, *Sunan Ibn Majah*²¹⁴, *Sunan Abu Dawud*²¹⁵ and *Jami' al-Tirmidhi*.²¹⁶

Typical of excellent military commanders then and now, Muhammad used deception as a normal feature of his military leadership. Al-Waqidi notes that "the Prophet of God never undertook a military action [lit. غزوة] without pretending that he was not doing so."²¹⁷ He kept preparations discrete, often informed leaders of the intended destinations via letters opened only after the parties had set off,²¹⁸ routinely sent his warriors to hide by day and travel by night,²¹⁹ told them to travel on unexpected or untrodden roads,²²⁰ and used ambushes on frequent occasions, particularly during the earlier small raids against mercantile caravans travelling north and south past Medina.

Raiding, a type of poaching, was a long-established, low-risk and low-casualty activity common within Arab society and was tied up in coming-of-age rites and widespread beliefs about the essential traits of manhood: daring, courage and élan. It should be seen as more akin to sport than the horrific activity that we today call war.²²¹ At its heart was cunning, not cruelty, and it had commonly understood "rules" that participants general adhered to, such as not killing non-fighters.

Muhammad's intuitive grasp of ruse is unmistakable. For instance, immediately after the Muslim defeat at the Battle of Uhud, the Prophet admonished a warrior named Sa'd ibn Abu Waqqas for shouting out his joy that the Quraysh were withdrawing to Mecca rather than raiding Medina. Knowing that this joy would make the Muslims look relieved, and therefore weak in the eyes of detractors, Muhammad told Sa'd: "Lower your voice. Indeed, war is deception. Do not show public joy that they have left."²²²

Despite the defeat, the next day Muhammad rode out with

his battered, exhausted but dedicated warriors — many of them wounded — ostensibly in pursuit of the victorious Quraysh. He did so in order to give the Quraysh the false impression that the Muslim army was unimpaired and in high morale so that they, the Quraysh, would not consider turning back to attack Medina.[223] In order to strengthen his ruse, Muhammad told his men to gather wood by day and to light a needlessly large number of fires at night.[224] He also had Maʿbad ibn Abu Maʿbad al-Khuzaʿi, a Bedouin who was secretly allied to him, go forward into the enemy camp with a tale that Muhammad was hot on their trail with a reinvigorated army "such as he had never seen".[225] This had the desired effect, and a nervous Abu Sufyan led his army directly back to Mecca.

When a powerful army of around 10,000 Quraysh warriors and allies marched upon Medina in 627 CE, for what became the Battle of the Trench, they commenced a lengthy siege. After around twenty-seven days, Muhammad sent Nuʿaym ibn Masʿud, a new convert to Islam, as a spy into the enemy camp to give faulty advice and sow discord between the enemy tribes. Unaware that Nuʿaym had converted to Islam, the Quraysh listened to his misinformation. Tired, oppressed by adverse weather and believing Nuʿaym's stories, the Quraysh eventually lost heart and withdrew, lifting the siege of Medina. Regarding this misinformation, Muhammad told his close confidante ʿUmar ibn al-Khattab that the ruse was his own idea, rather than a revelation from God, and that it had come to him because "war is deception".[226]

Interestingly, during that battle, Muhammad sent one of his friends, Hudhayfa ibn al-Yamam, to sneak into the enemy camp to gain information. Hudhayfa was undetected. He even sat at a campfire with the enemy leadership. He sat close enough to the commander, Abu Sufyan ibn Harb, to hear him explicitly warning his people against the likelihood of Muslim cunning or espionage and asking everyone to check who was sitting next to them.[227]

Later that year, during the campaign against the Banu Lihyan, Muhammad ordered his armies northward towards Syria to give the Banu Lihyan the impression that they were secure in the south.[228] Muhammad's army then circled back and attacked the enemy from the rear, threatening the tribe in its very encampments. As it happened, on this occasion Muhammad's ruse was unsuccessful and the Banu Lihyan managed to escape to the hills.

Six months later, when Muhammad wanted to undertake his minor pilgrimage to Mecca with unarmed followers, he responded to knowledge that the Quraysh would block the likely route into Mecca by leading his people through a narrow mountain path instead.[229]

Similarly, when planning his campaign against the troublesome people of Khaybar in May 628 CE, Muhammad again kept the destination secret, worrying that, if he disclosed it, the Ghatafan tribe allied to Khaybar might join the battle and provide overwhelming strength. He also advanced along certain routes that would ensure that the Ghatafan could not, even if they did hear, join with Khaybar.[230] Maintaining secrecy, he managed to catch the people of Khaybar unawares. Al-Waqadi relates that when the people of Khaybar opened their fortresses at dawn, carrying with them their farming implements for work, "they saw that the Messenger of God had arrived in their midst. They shouted, 'Muhammad and the army,' and turned and fled back into their fortresses."[231]

When planning the liberation of Mecca in January 630 CE, Muhammad even kept his closest advisors in the dark about his intentions until the very last minute so as to prevent the accidental leaking of information.[232] He then beseeched God for his military ruse to be successful with a prayer that almost perfectly sums up the meaning of his statement that "war is deception": "O Allah, hide all the signs [of preparation and advance] from the Quraysh and their spies until we can fall upon them with surprise."[233] A similar narration quotes him saying, "O Allah, take sight from the eyes of the Quraysh and do not let them see me or hear me until they do so unexpectedly."[234] As it happened, "not a word of the

Prophet's march reached the Quraysh."²³⁵

In the same campaign, Muhammad also cleverly used tactical ruse to gain psychological advantage. When night fell on the route they were taking he ordered every one of his ten thousand warriors to light a camp fire, thus giving the impression that his force was much larger than it actually was.²³⁶

Thus, even from this relatively small selection of the very many recorded examples of Muhammad's use of military deception, it is clear that he deployed it in a way that any objective scholar or practitioner of war would recognise and acknowledge as creative, reasonable and highly effective leadership.

In case any reader thinks that, by artfully leading military operations in such intelligent ways, Muhammad may have somehow actually enjoyed war, seeing it as a clever and skilful game to master, or had been casual about death, it is worth pointing out that he strongly disliked war and, as noted above, created strict rules about protecting the innocent. We can see some of these rules in his instructions to the army he despatched to Mu'tah in 629 CE:

> Attack in the name of Allah, and fight His enemy and yours in Al-Sham. You will encounter men [monks] secluded in monasteries, withdrawn from others. Do not attack them. You will find other people seeking out Satan and sin. Draw your swords against them. Do not kill a woman or a young child, or the old and unwell. Do not destroy the date palm, cut down trees, or destroy a dwelling ["بيت"].²³⁷

Thus, as well as the innocent, even infrastructure and the means of production were to be left alone. His use of the word بيت ("dwelling" or "house") makes it clear that he intended for family homes to be left untouched. We also know how he felt about the need to protect religious buildings. The Qur'an condemns the evil of destroying religious buildings, including Jewish synagogues:

الَّذِينَ أُخْرِجُوا مِن دِيَارِهِمْ بِغَيْرِ حَقٍّ إِلَّا أَن يَقُولُوا رَبُّنَا اللَّهُ وَلَوْلَا دَفْعُ اللَّهِ النَّاسَ بَعْضَهُم بِبَعْضٍ لَّهُدِّمَتْ صَوَامِعُ وَبِيَعٌ وَصَلَوَاتٌ وَمَسَاجِدُ يُذْكَرُ فِيهَا اسْمُ اللَّهِ كَثِيراً وَلَيَنصُرَنَّ اللَّهُ مَن يَنصُرُهُ إِنَّ اللَّهَ لَقَوِيٌّ عَزِيزٌ

[There are] those who have been evicted from their homes unjustly, only for saying, "Our Lord is Allah". And if it were not that Allah uses some people to counter others, then monasteries, churches, synagogues, and mosques would have been destroyed in which the name of Allah is much mentioned. And Allah will surely support those who support Him. Indeed, Allah is Powerful and Almighty.[238]

When trying to summarise Muhammad's ability to wield military might, one must admit that it is hard to compare his skills with those of history's legendary commanders, such as Alexander, Hannibal, Genghis Khan, Timur, Napoleon, Nelson, Lee, Rommel, and Patton. Warfare was as much a part of his life as it was of theirs. Yet his warfare did not resemble in scope, nature or purpose that bloody business prosecuted by those famous warriors.

Muhammad initiated around eighty "raids" — around eight a year for a decade — 27 of which he led himself[239], which might sound terribly aggressive and violent, but those raids did not always involve contact with an enemy and seldom caused casualties, let alone deaths. Many were only shows of force designed to demonstrate his community's increasing strength, to keep constant pressure on groups that might have allied with his enemies, to rustle from herds in accordance with existing social norms, and of course to take Islam to those who had not yet heard the message.

Even the "battles" were far less dramatic than they initially seem. Ibn Hisham and Al-Waqadi tell us that, if we exclude offensive and defensive sieges, in which almost no one died anyway, there were really only four pitched battles; that is, contact battles in which both sides used mass, maneuver and orchestrated violence on a battlefield. These may have had enormous social and political consequences, but they were also almost devoid of death. At Badr the Muslims suffered 14 dead; at Uhud 70; at Mu'tah 13 (from a force of 3,000) and at Hunayn (where Muhammad led 12,000 warriors) only four.[240] The deadliest siege undertaken by the Muslims, the assault on Khaybar, caused 15 Muslim deaths.[241] Even the famous Battle of the Trench, the basic aspects of which are known by most Muslims to this day, resulted in only six Muslim deaths.[242] The casualties they inflicted were not much greater. Indeed, if we add up casualties on both sides in the nine main confrontations spread throughout a decade of conflict, we can only count 138 dead Muslims and allies and 216 dead opponents.

We must therefore refrain from seeing Muhammad as violent or a warlord. He was probably only as engaged in war as any tribal sheikh in that period, and despite the frequent and dramatic sounding mentions of warfare that appear in the Qur'an and the ahadith, we would be wrong to see this activity through a modern lens. Rather than leaving battlefields littered with the nameless dead, as is now common in war, there were so few casualties in Muhammad's struggles that every single one is named in the sources.

The centrality of these military activities in Islamic origin stories owes a lot to the way that oral traditions which pass from generation to generation accentuate heroic deeds and noble qualities, which are ideal for weaving verbal spells in stories told around campfires. Muhammad has thus become the paradigmatic hero, much as Agamemnon, Achilles, and Odysseus did in Classical Greece.

If one wonders how good he actually was at this relatively bloodless activity that was far more about projecting confidence, power and a type of chiefly authority than about inflicting death and destruction, one must conclude that, in short, he was unusually capable and effective. Humane, courageous, creative, unhesitant, and utterly inspiring to his soldiers, he seemed always to know how best to keep pressure on his opponents and to stay one step ahead of them so that they always had to react to his moves without being able to implement their own plans. Exploiting speed, surprise and unity of command, he was able to move even large and tightly cohesive forces skilfully over long distances to impose his will on opponents with minimal losses on either side.

Maximising Human Potential

Muhammad believed not only in inspiring and motivating people, both in the peace he liked and the warfare he disliked, but also, through the thoughtful delegation of responsibilities. Through delegation he knew he could develop the confidence and capacity of people who seemed to possess potential for growth so that they might themselves move into leadership roles. He understood that delegation gave people senses of empowerment and motivation and that these would increase productivity and effectiveness because those who had been entrusted with tasks would work even harder than usual to prove that the trust in them had not been misplaced.

He saw delegation having four sequential phases: selecting, training, trusting, and rewarding. In other words, he constantly watched his people, especially the young and committed, looking for the potential in a person that he could build upon. When he saw someone with that extra spark, he brought that person close to him or to another elder so that, through example as well as direct engagement, he might help to train that person. Then, when he felt that person was ready to embrace responsibility, he would delegate a task to him. Sometimes, if he considered him ready, the task would be surprisingly large, complex and important.

It is worth analysing each of these steps in greater detail, beginning with how Muhammad spotted talent within his people. As noted above, he liked to get to know his people, watching them in the mosque, in their homes and in social interactions.

Sometimes they visited as house guests or as students. Some of his companions visited him on alternate days, and met to share what each had learned, so that they would not miss out on his teaching.[243] Malik ibn al-Huwayrith recalled: "We came to the Prophet ﷺ and stayed with him for twenty days and nights. We were all young and of about the same age. The Prophet ﷺ was very kind and merciful."[244]

Rather like Plato with his "Academy" and Aristotle with his "Lyceum", Muhammad created an informal peripatetic style of instruction, which involved not only intense sessions inside a home in Mecca (known as the "House of al-Arqam"), but also extensive talking, discussing and debating each day while walking with his companions and students.

He not only taught them but also watched them carefully, studying their interests, strengths and weaknesses. He looked to see their piety, creativity and intelligence, and later when warfare occurred he watched to see who possessed energy, courage and resolve.

During the Battle of the Trench, he urgently needed information about the enemy's movements. He called for a volunteer to undertake stealthy and dangerous reconnaissance behind enemy lines. One man, Zubayr ibn al-Awam, volunteered. To stress the danger of the task, the Prophet asked again for a volunteer. Zubayr stepped forward again. A third time he asked, and once again Zubayr volunteered. Delighted, the Prophet praised him publicly: "Every prophet has a disciple and my disciple is Zubayr!"[245]

He was always happy with those who worked hard to support his plans when they knew it involved discomfort or struggle. These were people to cultivate. Straight after the Battle of Uhud, which was Muhammad's first defeat, he called for volunteers to ride after the withdrawing opponents in a show of strength. "Who will go after them?" he called out.[246] This prompted a swell of enthusiasm, but he chose from among the volunteers only those who had fought the day before, not wanting any shirkers or cowards to pretend they were riding out bravely when in fact the enemy was already leaving.

Among those chosen by Muhammad were two brothers who had been badly wounded the day before. With only one mount between them, they were so keen to show him their worth that they took turns riding and walking.[247] He was naturally delighted to have warriors with such tenacity and fortitude.

Muhammad constantly looked to see among his people who had initiative, and sometimes asked, "Who will hear these words of mine, and then actually act upon them, or even teach them to someone who might act upon them?" (مَنْ يَأْخُذُ عَنِّي هَؤُلَاءِ الْكَلِمَاتِ فَيَعْمَلُ بِهِنَّ أَوْ يُعَلِّمُ مَنْ يَعْمَلُ بِهِنَّ). On the other hand, he did not like people to take on roles or tasks beyond their abilities[248], and he did not respect people who sought status and power for their own sake, rather than from a desire to serve. In a much quoted, and sometimes misquoted hadith, Muhammad told 'Abdur-Rahman ibn Samurah: "Do not seek leadership, because if you are given authority, then you will be held accountable for it, but if you are given it without asking for it, then you will be helped [by Allah]."[249]

Muhammad was not trying to diminish the marvelous spirit of volunteerism that always proves so beneficial within groups or organisations. He admired the genuine desire to serve that he often saw. He was really trying to say, as Aesop had once said: "be careful what you wish for". Leadership came with a heavy burden of responsibility, especially to be scrupulously just, and, as noted at the beginning of this analysis, "every shepherd will be asked about his treatment of his master's possessions," meaning both in this world and on Judgment Day.[250]

He understood that people learn best by doing. He often said that "when three [or more] people go on a journey, they should select a leader among them".[251] This seems an odd and excessive expectation, which some commentators explain away by saying that the Prophet meant a prayer leader; that is, that they should decide who among them was most expert in Qur'an and good conduct.

Muslims should indeed assign a prayer leader, but this is a limited reading of what Muhammad actually meant. More logically, he understood that any travel would require at least some administration and logistics and that — to learn essential skills that could later be built upon — responsibility for these matters should be apportioned to someone with apparent aptitude.

When caravan raids commenced shortly after the emigration to Medina, Muhammad himself commanded some of the missions. Each time he went he left a different person in charge of the believers in Medina, thus sharing out the ability for people to embrace responsibility, learn new skills or deepen their religiosity through service to the community. In short succession, to illustrate this point, he left Sa'd ibn Ubadah, Abu Salama ibn Abd al-Asad, and 'Abdullah ibn Ubayy in charge.

He was very keen to delegate to people even of a young age, seeing them as guileless, zealous, energetic, loyal and unswerving. For example, in 616 CE, when he sent a second group of around eighty Muslims to Abyssinia to seek asylum from King Armah during a period of persecution in Mecca, he placed them under the authority of Ja'far ibn Abi Talib. This young man, aged either 25 or 26, was far younger than most of the emigrants but he had served a thorough informal apprenticeship by learning directly from Muhammad, Abu Bakr and other elders. Ja'far was an inspired choice. When the Abyssinian king debated expelling the refugees, Ja'far spoke so eloquently and compellingly about the similarities between Muhammad's teachings and those of Christianity that the king agreed to provide them with asylum.[252]

A year before Muhammad left Mecca for Medina in 622 CE, twelve Medinans met him in Aqaba outside Mecca and pledged loyalty to him and obedience to his moral code. When they planned to return home, they requested that he send a representative to Medina in order to teach the Qur'an and invite people to Islam. Muhammad, then over fifty, could have sent one of his trusted comrades in his own age group. Instead he appointed Mus'ab ibn 'Umayr, recently returned from Abyssinia and then aged no more than 28, as Islam's first ambassador.[253] To Muhammad's distress, he died in the Battle of Uhud three years later.

After the opening of Mecca in 630 CE, Muhammad moved to defend his polity against forces massing against him. In his absence he needed to appoint a competent and trustworthy leader in Mecca, which had not yet become used to Islam. Despite having countless seasoned Muslims from whom to select, including his closest companions Abu Bakr, 'Umar ibn al-Khattab, 'Uthman ibn Affan and his son-in-law 'Ali ibn Abi Talib, Muhammad chose a 21-year-old young man named 'Attab ibn Asid, and asked him to pray with the people and act as steward.[254] He was in fact the first prayer leader (after Muhammad himself) to hold communal prayers in Mecca after its conquest. He was a fine administrator and leader and he remained in post in Mecca until well after Muhammad's death.

Similarly, when the people of Banu Thaqif of Ta'if converted to Islam in 630 CE, Muhammad appointed 'Uthman ibn Abu al-'As as their new leader, despite his youth, because of his reputation for piety. He saw something special in him, and was proven right. After justly governing Ta'if, 'Uthman ibn Abu al-'As served Muhammad's successors as governor of Bahrayn (eastern Arabia) and Oman (southeastern Arabia).

Muhammad was very fond of Usama ibn Zayd, the son of his adopted son Zayd ibn Harithah, and for many years used to have Usama ride behind him on his donkey.[255] He thus received very personal tuition. Muhammad even let Usama enter the Ka'ba with him, which was a rare privilege.[256] When he was fifteen, Usama fought in his first battle, wrongly killing an enemy solider who had uttered the Islamic confession of faith.[257] He was corrected by both Bashir ibn Sa'd, his patrol captain, and by the Prophet. Nonetheless, when Usama was nineteen, Muhammad advised him that he wanted to send him north as a military leader of a major expedition to avenge his father Zayd's death. This offended many of the older warriors and caused Muhammad publicly to put his foot down. Usama was ready and, indeed, he was suited for that mission.[258]

There was no nepotism or cronyism in Muhammad's decision. He simply believed that, although young, Usama was the right man for the job. Muhammad was, in fact, deeply opposed to delegating authority or responsibility, both large and small, to people who were unqualified or unworthy. Trusting people with oversight of issues when they were unqualified, he said, would be one of the signs of the Last Day.[259]

Abu Dharr al-Ghifari, a very early convert and a dear companion of the Prophet, once approached him with a request for an appointment to a public office. He hoped his friendship would secure the role, but Muhammad gently stroked his shoulder and explained that, because he perceived weakness, and responsibility required trust, he could not oblige. He added that on the Day of Judgment the apportionment of responsibilities would be a source of repentance and humiliation unless it involved the proper fulfilment of obligations.[260]

Likewise, when another man came to the Prophet and said "you appointed so-and-so, but you haven't appointed me to anything," Muhammad very gently and supportively told him that, in effect, he should accept what might for now seem like injustice, and that even leaders after him would pass the man over in favour of others, but that he should look for Muhammad on the Day of Judgment, when he might finally get his reward.[261] We do not know what weaknesses Muhammad had seen in him.

The appointment of a person to lead a detachment of troops was perhaps the most common form of delegation within Muhammad's community. The raids were ordinarily not as one might today imagine them: battles designed to kill and defeat enemies for political purposes. Rather, some were either small-scale surprise attacks on undefended or lightly defended caravans for material gain at a time when the Islamic polity was struggling financially and then equally small raids on Bedouins for livestock. Most were "shows of force" designed to gain control over certain roads or regions, to discourage groups from allying themselves with the Quraysh, to establish allies, or to convert the clans and the Bedouins.

A long-established part of Arab culture, such raids were hardly military in nature, and most involved small numbers of warriors, little fighting, and few or no deaths. The sources tell us that a particularly "fierce battle" occurred during Qutba ibn 'Amir ibn Hadida's raid, ordered by Muhammad, on a community from Khath'am in the Tabala region. Yet there were only twenty warriors in total, mounted on ten camels, so we need to keep in mind the small scale of such "battles".[262] Although small and light in casualties, they gave the Islamic polity invaluable experience and, when successful, increased prestige and authority. No wonder Muhammad saw them as an ideal apprenticeship for his young men.

Sometimes Muhammad selected these leaders purely because he saw potential that he wanted to develop, and other times he chose them because of their intimate local knowledge.[263] For example, he chose Ibn Abi al-'Awja al-Sulami to raid the Banu Sulaym, to which he had belonged, and Ghalib ibn 'Abdullah al-Laythi to fight the Banu al-Mulawwah of the Banu Layth, from which he had come.[264] The Prophet sent 'Amr ibn al-'As, although only a new convert, to lead a detachment against the Bali and the Quda'a because the Bali were maternal relatives and Muhammad hoped that 'Amr might be able to recruit from among them.[265]

Interestingly, 'Amr refused to let his warriors light a fire to keep back the cold, presumably because the fire would reveal their whereabouts. Some of the long-serving warriors argued back at him, doubtless bothered that a newcomer to Islam had received the Prophet's authority. But 'Amr had, and knew it. "You were ordered to listen to me and obey me," he said. "Do it."[266]

Muhammad embraced his responsibility to try to remedy flaws that he perceived within subordinates, recognising, of course, that change ultimately had to come from within. After the conversion of Khalid ibn al-Walid, the talented, fierce and fearless warrior whose cavalry charge into Muhammad's rear had caused his defeat at the Battle of Uhud, the Prophet was naturally pleased to have Khalid fighting on his side, and not against him. Yet he clearly saw that Khalid was, as he said of another fierce companion, Khirash ibn Umayya, "too prone to kill".[267] He understood that Khalid was a gifted and courageous fighter, which he could use if controlled, but that his aggression and innate tendency towards violence would need to be tempered outside of battle.

This initially proved to be a difficult task. After Khalid distinguished himself in the Battle of Mu'tah in 629 CE, Muhammad was upset when Khalid (like the aforementioned Khirash ibn Umayya) killed people during the liberation of Mecca in 630, a campaign that was supposed to be entirely bloodless. For some time after, Muhammad therefore sent Khalid out on other missions, not to fight, but to call tribes to Islam. This, Muhammad hoped, would teach him composure and patience. He nonetheless worried that Khalid might exceed bounds, and indeed on one occasion he did, when Muhammad sent him to the Banu Jadhima of Kinana.[268]

When the Banu Jadhima saw that Khalid was in their midst, they panicked and reached for their weapons. Khalid told them to lay down their weapons and that he would do them no harm. They quickly complied and surrendered their weapons, informing Khalid that they were in fact converts. Rejecting or misunderstanding this claim (they spoke a different dialect), Khalid bound them and had some executed. A number of Muhajirun and Ansar warriors in Khalid's force, who knew Muhammad's teachings on justice, directly disobeyed Khalid and refused to kill anyone, much to his annoyance. They knew that obedience was ordinarily essential. It was an Islamic teaching. But, as shown above, an act contrary to God's book or the Prophet had to be disobeyed. When Muhammad learned of Khalid's atrocity, he raised his hands to God and exclaimed, "O Allah I am innocent before You of what Khalid has done."[269] He then took out a loan[270] and sent 'Ali ibn Abi Talib with the money to make restitution with the Banu Jadhima, paying them blood money and compensation for everything damaged, right down to a dog's bowl. The outrage was so serious that 'Ali actually compensated them excessively, something Muhammad later commended.

When Khalid presented himself to Muhammad, the Prophet "turned away from Khalid and was angry at him," shunning him for a while to teach him the significance of his error. After two Muslim elders tried to reason with Khalid, causing him to remonstrate, Muhammad then rebuked him openly, telling him to be quiet and not to criticise companions, whose merits were worth twice any mountain of gold [lit. Mount Uhud] that Khalid could spend in God's service.[271] The heated displeasure of the Prophet was a serious rebuke and made Khalid change his ways.

Muhammad nonetheless knew that Khalid was an asset and that, if he could be controlled, he would become a great Muslim champion. He patiently persisted, working closely with Khalid to guide him before sending him out on further missions. Khalid still made mistakes, although never one as egregious as with the Banu Jadhima. During the Hunayn campaign, Muhammad came across a cluster of people gathered around the body of a slain woman. The Prophet sent someone to ask what had happened. When he returned and reported the woman's slaying, the Prophet exclaimed that women must never be killed. When he learned that Khalid was in charge of the responsible unit, Muhammad sent a messenger to instruct Khalid never to kill women.[272] This error notwithstanding, Khalid proved invaluable in the remaining years of Muhammad's life and later conquered Al-Sham (Greater Syria) in what most military historians consider a strategic triumph.

When Muhammad did empower subordinates to undertake certain tasks or responsibilities, he tried hard not to tie their hands but, more flexibly, to leave them with room for initiative and judgment. Granting subordinates the freedom to use their initiative does not mean that everyone did so. Some were less willing than others. When 'Umar led a raid against some of the Hawazin in 628, the opponents dispersed before his troop arrived. The Bedouin guide suggested that 'Umar instead make a raid on another nearby Bedouin group, which 'Umar declined to do because Muhammad had not explicitly authorised it.²⁷³ On another occasion the detachment leader, Abu Salama, faced exactly the same situation that 'Umar had, but when he realised that his enemy had dispersed, he sent two-thirds of his force to raid other groups and take spoils.²⁷⁴ The Prophet was happy with both decisions.

Al-Waqidi chronicles Muhammad's dispatch of Bashir ibn Sa'd and 300 warriors to Al-Jinab. When they arrived in the vicinity they came across a herd of cattle and discussed among themselves whether to appropriate the herd, which would mean they could not thereafter move with speed or surprise, or whether to continue against the enemy as they had been tasked. Using their initiative, they took the cattle, along with two prisoners, who converted and were freed by Muhammad.²⁷⁵ It was a successful mission.

Perhaps the best expression of the initiative imparted to those given tasks is the case of Mu'adh ibn Jabal to Yemen. When Muhammad sent him to serve as governor and to collect *zakat*, he asked him how he would settle any disputes.²⁷⁶ Mu'adh replied that he would rely on Qur'anic revelation. When Muhammad asked him what he would do if he could not find the answer he needed, Mu'adh said that he would rely on Muhammad's own example, and try to do what he knew the Prophet would do. When Muhammad probed further, asking what Mu'adh would do if he could not find a useful example, he said he would strive to apply his own judgment to the issue. Muhammad was delighted with the answer and fondly patted him on the chest.

Here we see an early expression of what Islamic scholars would later call *ijtihad* (اجتهاد), the independent mental struggle to find sound answers to questions apparently left unanswered by the Qur'an, the teachings and practices of Muhammad, and the consensus of scholars (إجماع, or *ijma*). Indeed, Muʿadh had used a form of the very word *ijtihad* when he explained his proposed method to Muhammad. He said: "ana ajtahidu" (قَالَ أَجْتَهِدُ); that is, that he would exert himself to find correct reasoning.

Here we see also the type of empowerment that today we call Mission Command or Directive Control, which means trusting one's trained and trusted subordinates to use their initiate to deliver the outcome they know the superior would want. This type of leadership promotes initiative and quick decision-making, within reasonable and clearly communicated and mutually understood constraints. The leader informs the subordinate of his intentions as well as the subordinate's own task and its context. Ideally, he says what is needed and why it is needed. Once away from the boss, the subordinate can then decide within his delegated freedom how best to achieve the task, keeping in mind what he knows or believes the boss would do if he were there.

This principle might be unusual in some cultures, but in Islam this was and still is entirely natural. Aside from the Qur'an itself, the Prophet's *Sunnah* (سُنَّة, example) guided all conduct, actions and habits. Everyone in Muhammad's community tried to emulate the way that he did both major and mundane things, not only because they wanted to garner his happiness, but also because they saw him as an ideal, seldom-erring person. Some Christians today use the slogan, WWJD, meaning "What would Jesus do?" to denote the moral imperative to act in a manner consistent with their messiah. For 1,400 years all Muslims have done this, with Muhammad's example being their object of focus as a core aspect of their religious understanding. This Sunnah found written expression a few centuries after his death in the vast corpus of ahadith and the normative body of laws and guidance that draw upon them.

Also importantly, when dispatching Muʿadh ibn Jabal to govern Yemen, Muhammad gave him guiding advice on how a good leader should always act. Clearly with shepherding and gentle care in mind, rather than exploitation or coercion which would inevitably cause antagonism, Muhammad said: "Make things easy and not difficult for the people, and give them good tidings and do not turn them against you."[277]

Muhammad believed in rewarding excellence or special effort, and gave distinguished contributors gifts of weapons, clothing, horses and camels, and even administrative functions (such as *zakat* gatherer) or leadership roles. A few examples will amply demonstrate this desire to reward.

As they marched to meet the Quraysh at Uhud in 625 CE, Muhammad rewarded Al-Hubab ibn Al-Mundhir, the companion who had, a year earlier in the Battle of Badr, advised him cleverly where to position his troops. Now he rewarded Al-Hubab with the honour of carrying the Khazraj banner into battle.[278]

In 627 CE, 'Abdullah ibn 'Umar fought alongside Muhammad in the Battle of the Trench when he was only fifteen, having been denied permission to fight at Badr two years earlier.[279] For his courage, and for ongoing service during the raid on the Banu Qurayza, Muhammad rewarded 'Abdullah in 629 with appointment as a *Qurra*, or communal Qur'an reciter.

During the Battle of Khaybar he hoped to find someone sufficiently meritorious to serve as a standard bearer. In an Arab army this was a great honour, and was ordinarily assigned to a proven leader. 'Ali ibn Abi Talib had initially been unable to fight because of an eye ailment, but he felt ashamed not to join Muhammad so he took his place in battle despite his eye problems. Muhammad was moved and impressed, and duly bestowed upon 'Ali the honour of carrying the flag.[280]

After Khalid ibn al-Walid's heroism and selflessness in the Battle of Mu'tah, when he held aloft the Muslim flag and rallied troops to it on his own initiative after three other flag-bearers had been killed[281], Muhammad bestowed upon him a reward so great that it has survived for 1,400 years: his title as the "Sword of Allah".[282]

When new Meccan converts fought in the Battle of Hunayn and thus proved their loyalty at a time when some of Muhammad's advisors expressed concern about their sincerity, he rewarded them with unusually large numbers of camels.[283]

When 'Abdullah ibn Anys returned from a mission to kill Khalid ibn Sufyan ibn Nubayh al-Hudhali, a bitter and intransigent foe who was raising a force against Muhammad, the Prophet rewarded him with the gift of a staff, telling him: "It will be a sign between you and me on Resurrection Day". 'Abdullah ibn Anys was so moved by this gift that he kept it close throughout his life and had it enclosed in his shroud when he was buried.[284]

Muhammad was both people and task focused, and sometimes became disappointed when a task was left incomplete, especially if he believed it was manageable by the team he assigned, even if not by the leader himself. He wanted to see initiative. After one military patrol failed, he said with frustration: "When I send out a man who does not fulfil my commands, are you unable to appoint in his place one who will fulfil my commands?"[285]

He did not like having to chase people to do something he had asked them. If he asked for something to be done, he only liked to ask once. He also wanted it done right, completed to the degree he had asked.[286] When he asked Khalid ibn Al-Walid to destroy the shrine to the pagan goddess al-'Uzza, the latter returned and confirmed that he had done as requested. Muhammad inquired what he had done, but was unhappy with the answer. "Surely you have not destroyed it, so go back and do it right this time."[287]

Yet he was very tolerant of mistakes, and is not known to have rebuked anyone for lack of success, even in the military sphere, if they had shown genuine effort. As he said: "When I ask you to do something, do it as best [lit. as much as] you can."[288] If results were imperfect but the effort was genuine, he never criticised. He believed that it was "better for a leader to make a mistake in forgiving than to make it in punishing."[289]

He also taught that Muslims should not publicly disclose each other's faults, but, to protect the dignity of those who had erred or failed, should always "cover" them; that is, keep them unspoken. He said: "Whoever covers the faults of a brother, Allah will cover his on the Day of Judgment."[290] He strictly practiced what he preached. Anas ibn Malik, a young man who was for Muhammad what we would today call a personal assistant, recalled: "I served the Prophet for ten years. He never said *Uff* [an expression of disgust] and never blamed me by saying: 'Why did you do so?' or why did you not do so?'"[291]

When his army returned from a defeat in Mu'tah, many of the Medinans crowded the streets and mocked and jeered at them for failing. Some even threw dirt at them. Muhammad, on the other hand, was quick to stop this maltreatment, telling the people: "They have not fled the battlefield. They will return if God wills it."[292]

He was also remarkably forgiving when disobeyed, which certainly did not happen often, but cases can be found in the earliest sources. This is not surprising given that even Moses's people had disobeyed him. Many humans are weak, foolish and disobedient by nature and even a prophet in their midst was not always enough to transform them. Al-Waqidi records that, when Muhammad signed the Treaty of Hudaybiyyah, his followers were initially unable to grasp its strategic significance and saw it as a humiliation. Resentful and angry, they refused his order to shave their heads and slaughter the sacrificial animals.[293] He was deeply upset, but he could not get them to comply with his instructions until, as an example to them (on his wife Umm Salama's advice), he had his own head shaved and his animals slaughtered. Ashamed, they finally did as they were told. Conveying a revelation that the treaty was in fact a great victory, he forgave them totally with no residual bad feelings.

Similarly, before the advance on Mecca in 630 CE the Prophet demanded total secrecy, as noted above. One man, Hatib ibn Abu Balta'a, nonetheless dispatched an informer to Mecca to warn them of Muhammad's plans.²⁹⁴ The informer was intercepted, and Muhammad summoned Hatib. He begged for forgiveness, explaining that he had disobeyed the Prophet out of fear for his son and family who still resided in Mecca without any powerful family connections that might protect them. Muhammad was moved, and forgave Hatib.

That does not mean that he tolerated disobedience among those entrusted with major tasks. He is known to have dismissed appointees if they strayed without reason from clear instructions. During the march on Mecca he insisted firmly and repeatedly that he wanted to take the city without bloodshed. When he learned that Sa'd ibn Ubadah, one of the leaders of the four powerful columns advancing upon Mecca, had publicly stated that this was war so there would be no quarter given, Muhammad immediately relieved him of command.²⁹⁵

Muhammad was also intolerant of anything less than scrupulously moral conduct, and, as Khalid ibn al-Walid's case above shows, he made it publicly clear when he was upset at someone's misconduct. During the Battle of Khaybar, he was especially bothered to find hidden in the saddle cloth of one warrior more than the man was entitled to as spoils. He did not punish him physically but he treated him harshly and publicised his guilt.²⁹⁶

He was especially intolerant of immoral behaviour in anyone in a position of responsibility. He said: "Whoever from among you is appointed by us to a position of authority, and he conceals from us even a needle or something smaller, it will be misappropriation and he will have to account for it on the Day of Judgement."²⁹⁷ At one point he appointed a man called Ibn al-Utbiyyah to collect the charity required of the Banu Sulaym. When he arrived back in Medina he announced to the Prophet all the wealth he had gathered, and then presented him with a gift that he said he had himself received as a gift. Muhammad was furious both that Ibn al-Utbiyyah had taken a personal gift while gathering the charity and that he presumed Muhammad would take something for himself. He therefore stood on the minbar, the pulpit in the mosque, and exclaimed:

> What is the matter with this collector of sadaqah? We sent him out and when he returns he says: "This is for you and it's is a present which was given to me." … Whoever takes any of the charity will inevitably bring it with them on the Day of Resurrection, whether it is a camel which growls, an ox which bellows, or a sheep which bleats.[298]

Then stretching out his arms, he said: "O Allah, haven't I made myself clear? O Allah, haven't I made myself clear?"

Muhammad understood that egregious wrongdoing could not go unpunished and he was especially resolute in publicly punishing anyone who threated the cohesion of his community. During the Battle of Uhud, for instance, Al-Harith ibn Suwayd al-Samit, a Muslim fighter from the Banu Aws, used the smokescreen of the chaos of combat to kill Al-Mujadhdhar al-Dhiyad al-Balawi, a Muslim fighter from the Banu Khazraj, as revenge in a blood feud.[299] When Muhammad learned of this despicable act, which represented the worst of the old tribal system that Islam replaced, as well as a lack of honour in putting personal issues ahead of the common good during a time of crisis, he had the men of Al-Harith's local mosque arranged into lines, and then spoke to them about the wrongdoing. Al-Harith pleaded for forgiveness, claiming that Satan had seduced him into the act and even promising to pay the blood money, to undertake two months of fasting, to free a slave and to feed sixty poor people. Muhammad remained unmoved. He was appalled by the crime of a Muslim killing a Muslim and knew he had to demonstrate clearly that the Islamic community now superseded all tribalism. He ordered Al-Harith's execution, which was duly carried out.

Diplomatic Leadership

Just as we cannot attribute a modern understanding of strategy to Muhammad without imposing serious anachronism — attributing concepts and theories used now but certainly not known in the seventh century — we cannot use a modern diplomatic framework to understand how he negotiated agreements with other communities, tribes and polities.

Nowadays we see diplomacy as the art of conducting negotiations between specialised representatives ("diplomats") of states. This involves: the presentation and advocacy of the state's position; negotiation; bargaining; and other discourse to advance the state's foreign policy goals.

Muhammad lived in an era before states. The recognised polities — the distinct social organisations throughout Arabia — included oases and towns of various sizes which often held influence over surrounding areas of varying extent; tribes and clans of different size and power which sometimes existed alone or with other tribes and clans within those towns; and groups of semi-nomadic pastoral Arabs living with their herds in the gaps elsewhere. Each polity organised itself through its own common identity, which was ordinarily a sense of kinship or genealogical connection, little hierarchy (except for non-hereditary leaders), and the capacity to acquire resources (often through trade but sometimes through raids) and then mobilise them for the optimal wellbeing of the people. All these groups were interdependent, meaning that none could really survive without at least some trade with the other groups, yet they had little else to hold them together and they certainly had no sense of being "a people".

Nowadays, diplomats are representatives of state governments. Muhammad created a type of governance — meaning he created, articulated and enforced religious, ethical, social, cultural and economic norms — but he had no state and he had no government in any recognised modern sense. At most, we can say that he created an ever-enlarging *umma* (community) that, in its area of influence, superseded the traditional family-and-clan-based tribal structure, yet which itself looked and functioned more as a tribe than what we today call a state. And Muhammad's own role was more akin to that of a tribal sheikh than to any of the head of state roles we would today recognise, such as king, president, prime minister, chancellor or even supreme leader.

Yet Muhammad, who wielded tremendous power and influence across a large part of Arabia by the time of his death in 632, only a decade after gaining his first taste of what today we might call political authority as a mediator in Medina, had to form relationships and alliances with neighbouring tribes, groups, town and other polities. It was a major part of his leadership.

Perhaps we might call these activities diplomacy, without trying to push the term into the domain of inappropriate anachronism. It is clear that, whatever we call these activities, Muhammad was exceptionally good at them and adept at seeing opportunities, manipulating circumstances, advancing interests, and achieving beneficial results. As a leader, this was one of his great abilities.

As noted above, at the heart of Muhammad's concept of leadership was the bay'a, the obedience pledge that bound people together, ordinarily with one agreeing to listen to and obey the other in return for protection, care and even reward. This concept lay at the heart of his diplomacy. In short, he envisaged all tribes, clans, and other groups being bound to him, as God's messenger and instrument for creating a just and pious world, through pledges of loyalty and obedience. This, he believed, would create a world of piety, stability, cohesion, and safety. To achieve this, he reached out to other groups inside and beyond Arabia, aiming to create a God-fearing world.

Today many scholars of diplomacy argue, as Hans J. Morgenthau opined, that the key aspects of diplomacy include: establishing objectives based on a realistic assessment of actual and real capacity and power; determining those very things in other polities; determining the extent to which these align or differ; establishing strategies and courses of action for increasing alignment and decreasing differences. To undertake diplomacy effectively, according to Morgenthau and many modern commentators, the diplomatic process has three tools available to it: persuasion, compromise, and coercion (meaning the threat of force or painful penalties).[300]

Muhammad never conceptualised his diplomatic aims and activities in this fashion, and, indeed, may never have consciously mapped them out in any way resembling a blueprint or even a plan. But he did have a clear end state in mind and he possessed an innate, intuitive aptitude for getting other communities and peoples to do as he wanted. At various times he did everything that modern theorists consider the key tenets of diplomacy, and he used all three of the aforementioned tools.

He clearly hoped he could usually achieve his aims through persuasion, which sits at the center of every diplomatic effort. He believed that the truths within Islam were self-evident and that, if he could get this message out to other communities they might embrace it on the basis of its reasonableness and its promise of spiritual rewards.

In particular after the Treaty of Hudaybiyyah and the subsequent success at Khaybar had established his legitimacy and significant authority, Muhammad sent out written invitations to leaders of communities inside and beyond Arabia.

Extending the hospitality and generosity that were customary and expected of sheikhs within Arab society, he also welcomed to

Medina many delegations from tribes, clans and nomadic groups who wished to pledge to him or at least to listen to his viewpoint. He extended them safe passage and welcome. Not all became Muslim, but all who entered agreements returned home with guarantees of safety and cooperative coexistence, with a requirement to pay *zakat* if they became Muslim or *jizya* if they did not.

A clear example of the diplomacy embedded in his interaction with these delegations can be found in the case of the Christians of Najran, a town in southwestern Arabia just north of Yemen. Muhammad sent them a letter, delivered by Khalid ibn al-Walid and 'Ali ibn Abi Talib. It had no real impact, so Muhammad sent a messenger to explain Islam.

In response, the Christians sent to Medina a delegation of sixty people, including scholars, to meet Muhammad.[301] With Muhammad's blessing they prayed in the mosque, facing east rather than towards Mecca.[302] This may have been the first time that Christians ever prayed in a mosque. Despite the bond of monotheism and his best efforts, Muhammad and the Christians were not able to reach common ground on some theological issues, yet he remained a hospitable host, providing sustenance and accommodation.

Although both sides failed to convince the other, they nevertheless worked out a mutually acceptable relationship. The Christians would provide two thousand garments a year, to be supplied twice annually, along with the loan of armour and weapons should a war with Yemen occur. In return, Muhammad guaranteed secure co-existence, cordial relations and guarantees of full religious freedom without molestation or interference.[303] The Christians also requested that Muhammad send with them a wise man who could serve as an adjudicator. Wanting this prestigious appointment, several of Muhammad's companions hoped they would be picked, with 'Umar stretching himself to full height when Muhammad scanned the mosque, hoping he would be noticed. Muhammad instead chose Abu 'Ubaydah ibn al-Jarrah.[304]

Being unable to conduct all diplomacy in person, Muhammad constantly sent out *rusul* (رُسُل, messengers) to Arabian and external polities, both great and small, powerful and weak, settled and nomadic. These were not diplomats in a modern sense who could negotiate independently on behalf of a known policy. Rather, they carried the spiritual message of Islam and written and verbal statements affirming Muhammad's prophethood and hopes of happy and mutually beneficial coexistence, ideally within the framework of Islam, but through non-aggression agreements if not. He expected these messengers not to be harmed and, in a spirit of reciprocity, he never imprisoned or harmed the messengers of other polities.[305]

This later developed in Islamic jurisprudence into a doctrine called *aman* (أمان), or "diplomatic immunity".[306] To Muhammad, a Muslim messenger sent elsewhere remained his representative, and therefore still under his protection, and a representative coming to him on behalf of another community was a guest, with rights granted by Arab custom, and was likewise under his protection. He took this very seriously, saying: "Whoever kills a person granted the assurance of protection will not smell the fragrance of Paradise even though it can be smelled at a distance of forty years [of travel]."[307]

He believed in this right to safety so firmly that when he heard (incorrectly) that his own emissary to Mecca had been killed during the pilgrimage attempt that led to the Treaty of Hudaybiyyah, he was so appalled that he had his followers pledge their willingness to march on Mecca if needed, regardless of the outcome that God would decide.[308]

Muhammad ordered his diplomatic messengers to be resolute in pursuit of political arrangements, but also to deliver the religious message sweetly. After all, in the Qur'an, believers were exhorted to be gentle with the sharing of its message:

ادْعُ إِلَى سَبِيلِ رَبِّكَ بِالْحِكْمَةِ وَالْمَوْعِظَةِ الْحَسَنَةِ وَجَادِلْهُم بِالَّتِي هِيَ أَحْسَنُ

$$\text{إِنَّ رَبَّكَ هُوَ أَعْلَمُ بِمَن ضَلَّ عَن سَبِيلِهِ وَهُوَ أَعْلَمُ بِالْمُهْتَدِينَ}$$

Call to the way of your Lord with wisdom and fair exhortation, and argue with them in the best way possible. Your Lord surely knows best who has gone astray from His way, and He knows best who are the rightly guided.[309]

The Qur'an also says that God even instructed Moses to bring the message gently to the Pharaoh:

$$\text{فَقُولَا لَهُ قَوْلاً لَّيِّناً لَّعَلَّهُ يَتَذَكَّرُ أَوْ يَخْشَى}$$

And speak to him with gentle words, so that he might become mindful or even feel some awe.[310]

Initially Muhammad had little to offer other tribes and groups except for the spiritual benefits that came with Islam, but after he began to consolidate power and even some wealth from 622 onwards, he was able to sweeten his offers. He offered inducements that were sometimes sufficient to tempt other communities into ending their independence or their alliances with Mecca and then, entering into the fold of Islam or, failing that, negotiating peaceful coexistence agreements.

One means of achieving this was to allocate shares in the spoils taken during a raid or battle. Increasingly substantial military victories, particularly major successes such as the Battle of Hunayn, gave him the ability to attract or retain the loyalty of various groups who understood that accepting Islam or at least Muhammad's authority could bring not only spiritual benefits, but also earthly rewards. Already mentioned above was the unusually generous share of booty given to Abu Sufyan ibn Harb, his sons and other newly converted Meccan dignitaries as a means of "winning over their hearts".[311]

One bitter and longtime enemy of Muhammad, a polytheist named Safwan ibn Umayya, fled to Yemen from Mecca when Muhammad's army entered, only returning when he had been promised safety. He remained a polytheist, asking Muhammad for two months' grace to consider his options. Despite knowing that Safwan had previously organised and funded warfare against him, Muhammad replied that he could have four months. Muhammad shrewdly courted this stubborn opponent, asking him for a loan of armour and weapons. Safwan asked if he had to do so, to which Muhammad replied that it was merely a friendly request and that Safwan would get his possessions back. He consented. Muhammad then went further, ingeniously inviting Safwan to fight with the Muslims in the Battles of Hunayn and Ta'if. Safwan agreed. After massive spoils fell into Muhammad's hands, he noticed that Safwan was admiring the large herds of cattle and sheep that were passing before him. Muhammad asked him if he like what he saw. The polytheist replied that indeed he did, to which Muhammad replied that they were all his, with no strings attached. Safwan immediately converted to Islam.[312]

One might see these inducements as evidence that submission to Muhammad, or conversion to Islam, was insincere, based only on the tangible benefits to be gained by doing so. Muhammad certainly encouraged sincerity, knowing it was a godly quality praised in the Qur'an. He strongly disliked insincerity. Yet he was also pragmatic. He seems not to have judged the motives, leaving that privilege to God, preferring instead to accept the actions. As he sometimes said regarding this very matter, "I am not ordered to look into the hearts of men."[313] He sensibly understood that he could far more easily work on transforming their beliefs once they were inside the community, rather than if they remained outside.

Often when delegations met with him in Medina, he rewarded those who accepted Islam with valuable "prizes" (الجوائـز), such as gifts of silver.[314] He had a standard "prize" amount, which he asked Bilal to give to all those in the delegations who converted, but he sometimes gave extra if he heard that someone came from a poor tribe or lacked money for the return trip. Modern critics might see this as an unpalatable or at least an unusual thing to do, but it accords with the Qur'anic revelation that rewarding faith in material ways will strengthen the faith and create long-lasting gratitude. In political terms, this will lead to ongoing loyalty.

When Abraham came to Mecca, the Qur'an says that he prayed to God that, when his struggling offspring offered prayers, they would be rewarded with food so that their hearts would be transformed and they would remain grateful.

رَبَّنَا إِنِّي أَسْكَنتُ مِن ذُرِّيَّتِي بِوَادٍ غَيْرِ ذِي زَرْعٍ عِندَ بَيْتِكَ الْمُحَرَّمِ رَبَّنَا لِيُقِيمُواْ الصَّلاَةَ فَاجْعَلْ أَفْئِدَةً مِّنَ النَّاسِ تَهْوِي إِلَيْهِمْ وَارْزُقْهُم مِّنَ الثَّمَرَاتِ لَعَلَّهُمْ يَشْكُرُونَ

> Our Lord, I have settled some of my offspring in an uncultivable valley near Your [sacred] house. Our Lord, so that they may establish the prayers, and that their hearts will incline towards them, provide them with fruits, so that they may become grateful.[315]

Muhammad's "reward" system may have represented inducement, which is a very respectful diplomatic method of winning people who might otherwise need different reasons for reaching agreement than purely intellectual persuasion, but it was certainly not bribery; money paid to induce some type of unethical conduct. Indeed, the early source reveal no examples of Muhammad ever offering bribes, much less for something immoral.

Muhammad did not compromise on religious matters, but he often did so in diplomatic matters, such as his acceptance of the Treaty of Hudaybiyyah, in order to achieve a win-win solution, even if it meant forsaking short-term goals. He recognised that stubbornness and dogmatism were unhelpful within negotiations, and he sometimes yielded ground or softened his demands. The fact that his negotiations often resulted in non-aggression agreements rather than the other party's acceptance of Islam demonstrate that he could accept partial instead of total accomplishment in the short-term. Oddly, many states today make concessions to another only when they are weak. Yet Muhammad the diplomat often did so during his years of strength. He astutely understood that, if people were going to honour their agreements, there was more likelihood of this occurring if they felt that they had been fairly treated by the Prophet and felt heard by him. Of course, it goes even further. Muhammad knew that God did not want him to coerce people into embracing Islam. The Qur'an was clear: "There is no compulsion in religion." (لَا إِكْرَاهَ فِي الدِّينِ)[316]

Although it might not be evident to many readers, in *Surah al-Tawba* the Qur'an itself actually refers to a significant act of humane and merciful diplomatic compromise that Muhammad was required to undertake: the honouring of pilgrimage promises of hospitality and protection in Mecca that the Quraysh had made to pagans. We do not know with whom or how any negotiations occurred. But that this happened is clear from the Qur'an, which stressed in another chapter that the breaking of contractual obligations was strictly prohibited: "O you who believe, fulfil your contracts" (يَا أَيُّهَا الَّذِينَ آمَنُوا أَوْفُوا بِالْعُقُودِ).[317] Indeed, the longest single verse in the Qur'an (*Surah al-Baqarah* 2.282) covers this very subject of oaths and contracts.

Surah al-Tawba 9:5, often called "the Verse of the Sword," seems an unusually violent pronouncement for a prophet who had preached tolerance, peace and reconciliation. Yet it is equally true that, when read in the context of the verses above and below verse 9:5, and when the circumstances of its revelation by Muhammad are considered, it is not difficult for readers to understand that it involves, as an act of political compromise, a period of grace for unbelievers who possessed existing agreements with the Quraysh. This is the Verse of the Sword:

فَإِذَا انسَلَخَ الأَشْهُرُ الْحُرُمُ فَاقْتُلُواْ الْمُشْرِكِينَ حَيْثُ وَجَدتُّمُوهُمْ وَخُذُوهُمْ وَاحْصُرُوهُمْ وَاقْعُدُواْ لَهُمْ كُلَّ مَرْصَدٍ فَإِن تَابُواْ وَأَقَامُواْ الصَّلاَةَ وَآتَوُاْ الزَّكَاةَ فَخَلُّواْ سَبِيلَهُمْ إِنَّ اللَّهَ غَفُورٌ رَحِيمٌ

Then when the sacred months have passed, slay the pagans wherever you find them, and seize them, and besiege them, and sit in wait for them in every place [of ambush]. …

The fact that the verse actually starts with the Arabic adverb "fa," translated here as "then," indicates that its line of logic flows from the verse or verses above it. Indeed, the preceding four verses explain the context.

Verse 1 gives the historical context as a violation of the Treaty of Hudaybiyyah. Two years after the treaty was signed, the Banu Bakr tribe, which had allied with the Quraysh, attacked the Banu Khuza'a tribe, which had joined the side of the Muslims. Muhammad correctly considered the attack to be a treaty violation, aware that an attack on an ally technically constituted an attack on his own community.[318] He could not let it pass. Nor did he want to. It was not a case of allowing the misbehaviour of a minor ally to force his hand, but he saw the necessity of demonstrating to his other allies than he would always honour his alliances with them. He therefore occupied Mecca peacefully and purified the Ka'ba (destroying no fewer than 360 idols inside it).

Regarding this period of purification, the Qur'anic revelation contained a very stern warning, that anyone wanting to undertake polytheistic pilgrimages to Mecca, or continue immoral rituals within it, should understand that henceforth they would not be permitted to do so. No polytheism and idolatry would ever again be tolerated within Islam's holy city. From that time on, it would be a city devoted to Allah alone. As *Surah al-Tawbah* 9:17 and 18 says:

مَا كَانَ لِلْمُشْرِكِينَ أَن يَعْمُرُواْ مَسَاجِدَ اللهِ شَاهِدِينَ عَلَى أَنفُسِهِمْ بِالْكُفْرِ أُوْلَئِكَ حَبِطَتْ أَعْمَالُهُمْ وَفِي النَّارِ هُمْ خَالِدُونَ

إِنَّمَا يَعْمُرُ مَسَاجِدَ اللهِ مَنْ آمَنَ بِاللهِ وَالْيَوْمِ الآخِرِ وَأَقَامَ الصَّلاَةَ وَآتَى الزَّكَاةَ وَلَمْ يَخْشَ إِلاَّ اللهَ فَعَسَى أُوْلَئِكَ أَن يَكُونُواْ مِنَ الْمُهْتَدِينَ

It is not fitting for idolaters to be in Allah's mosques, since they have witnessed against themselves with unbelief. ...

Allah's mosques should be only for those who believe in Allah and the Last Day, who observe prayer and give charity and fear none but Allah ....

Verses 2 and 3 were revealed through Muhammad to give the polytheists or idolaters then staying in Mecca and its environs as well as any polytheistic or idolatrous pilgrims in transit along Muslim-controlled trade and pilgrimage routes a clear warning that they should desist or leave. The scriptures generously included a period of amnesty — honouring agreements the pagans had made with the Quraysh tribe — that would last until the end of the current pilgrimage season. Thus, as an act of time-bounded political compromise, Muhammad gave Arab polytheists and idolaters in Mecca a four-month period of grace.

Verse 4 makes clear that during that period of amnesty, polytheists or idolaters already in Mecca were to be left untouched so that Muslims would not themselves become promise-breakers:

فَأَتِمُّواْ إِلَيْهِمْ عَهْدَهُمْ إِلَى مُدَّتِهِمْ إِنَّ اللهَ يُحِبُّ الْمُتَّقِينَ

So fulfil your treaties with them to the end of their term; indeed, Allah loves the righteous.

After clarifying that the threatened violence would apply only to those who then ignored the warnings and continued to practice polytheism or idolatry in and around the holy city and its sanctuary, and were still foolish enough not to have left after the four months, verse 5 — the sword verse — clearly warned them that there would be an armed purging or purification in which they clearly risked being killed.

The verse actually has a secondary clause which, after the direction to root out and kill anyone who had ignored the clear and solemn warnings and continued their polytheism or idolatry in the sacred city, enjoined Muslims to remember that they must be merciful ("to open the way", فَخَلُّوا سَبِيلَهُمْ) to those who repented and accepted their penitent obligations in terms of Islam. Moreover, the Verse of the Sword is immediately followed by an unusually charitable verse in which any of the pagans who asked for protection or immunity in case of any future violence were not only to be excluded from that violence, but were to be escorted to a place of safety.

وَإِنْ أَحَدٌ مِّنَ الْمُشْرِكِينَ اسْتَجَارَكَ فَأَجِرْهُ حَتَّى يَسْمَعَ كَلَامَ اللَّهِ ثُمَّ أَبْلِغْهُ مَأْمَنَهُ ذَلِكَ بِأَنَّهُمْ قَوْمٌ لاَّ يَعْلَمُونَ

> If anyone among the pagans asks you for protection, grant it to him, so that he might understand the words of Allah, then escort him to a place of safety. That is because they are people who do not know [the truth]. [319]

The rest of Surah 9 contains more explanation for the Muslims as to why they would now need to fight, and fight fiercely, anyone who broke their oaths or violated the sanctity of holy places, despite earlier hopes for peace according to the terms of the Treaty of Hudaybiyyah and the *bay'a* made to Muhammad when he entered Mecca. Clearly, this verse was not requiring violence against all unbelievers, but only those who exceeded their existing diplomatic agreements, as Verses 11 and 12 makes clear:

فَإِن تَابُواْ وَأَقَامُواْ الصَّلاَةَ وَآتَوُاْ الزَّكَاةَ فَإِخْوَانُكُمْ فِي الدِّينِ وَنُفَصِّلُ الآيَاتِ لِقَوْمٍ يَعْلَمُونَ

وَإِن نَّكَثُواْ أَيْمَانَهُم مِّن بَعْدِ عَهْدِهِمْ وَطَعَنُواْ فِي دِينِكُمْ فَقَاتِلُواْ أَئِمَّةَ الْكُفْرِ إِنَّهُمْ لاَ أَيْمَانَ لَهُمْ لَعَلَّهُمْ يَنتَهُونَ

> Yet if they repent and establish prayers and pay the charity, they are your brothers in religion. And We explain in detail Our revelations for people seeking knowledge.

> But if they break their oaths after their agreement and defame your religion, then fight the leaders of unbelief — their oaths are nothing — so that they may cease.

The fact that Muhammad favoured persuasion but could also employ compromise in diplomatic matters, as this case shows, does not mean that he ever shied away from applying diplomatic coercion. Sending a messenger to Fadak at the time when he was besieging Khaybar was certainly such an act of coercive diplomacy. Fadak was quick to reach a settlement with him.

The very march on Mecca in 630 was also entirely diplomatically coercive, a fact that cannot be disguised by the fact that it was also bloodless. When the Banu Bakr, allied with the Quraysh, attacked the Banu Khuza'a, allied with the Muslims, Abu Sufyan ibn Harb, the Quraysh leader, rode at once to Muhammad in Medina, imploring him not to hold this against the Quraysh and asking to reaffirm the Treaty of Hudaybiyyah. With great skill, Muhammad retained the moral high ground while rebuffing his nervous counterpart.

Muhammad then began to assemble a massive army of 10,000 Medinan and allied warriors to lead towards Mecca, at a time when Mecca — which had lost many allies to the Muslim side and was running short of food now that Muslims and their allies controlled most of the areas and roads around Mecca[320] — was militarily unable to resist. This cannot be seen as anything but the cleverly worked-out threat of force to compel the Meccan leadership into handing the sacred precinct over to the Muslim polity. In other words, Muhammad created in his opponents the expectation of costs of sufficient magnitude to break their motivation to continue their opposition to his desire for religious reform.

Muhammad had long dreamed of liberating Mecca and worked tirelessly to develop, through artful diplomacy with other tribes and groups, sufficient strength to make his threat seem imminent, entirely believable and utterly irresistible. Aware of the buildup, Abu Sufyan retuned to him a second time, now to negotiate a settlement.

Muhammad made it clear that he would accept nothing less than the end of polytheism in Mecca. Aware that Muhammad was unstoppable, Abu Sufyan negotiated the surrender of Mecca. Muhammad had thus outmaneuvered the Meccan leadership with masterful statesmanship, forcing it to submit to his will without the use of force.

It needs to be said that no religious coercion occurred. Even when the assembled Meccans swore their bay'a to Muhammad in front of the Ka'ba, they were not made to become Muslims. Many chose to do so of their own volition, and in coming days and weeks even more did so.

While critics of Islam insist that Muhammad did coerce Arab tribes and groups religiously, and not merely diplomatically, they cannot fail to observe that many of the detachments of troops that he sent out had no military purpose and caused no deaths. Rather, they were either *Da'wah* missions (دعوة, calling people to Islam) or shows of strength designed to demonstrate to tribal leaders that he possessed genuine power and that they might do well to ally themselves with him. The detachment leaders issued both a call to Islam and a coercive threat that, if they would not submit to Muhammad's authority, fighting would follow. At first sight, the early sources do seem to support this. For example, Ibn Hisham tells us that, a few months after the fall of Mecca,

> The messenger sent Khalid ibn al-Walid ... to the Banu al-Harith ibn Ka'b in Najran, and ordered him to invite them to Islam three days before he attacked them. If they accepted then he was to accept it from them; and if they declined he was to fight them. ... So Khalid set out and came to them, and sent out riders in all directions inviting the people to Islam, saying, "if you accept Islam you will be safe," so the men accepted Islam as they were invited.[321]

Yet a very clear distinction needs to be made between succumbing to the diplomatic coercion to accept Muhammad's authority and enter into political alliance with him — which did not require the embrace of Muhammad's religion — and any notions of forced conversion, which Muhammad stood steadfastly against. Any group or tribe could simply perform bay'a, that is, pledge political loyalty to Muhammad and agree not to join alliances against him, at which point no fighting would occur and the besieged could keep their religion.[322] All they needed to do was agree to pay their tax to Muhammad's polity as *jizya*, rather than as *zakat*.

According to several ahadith, Muhammad explained to the leaders of detachments that he sent out to expand the polity and its tax-based wealth (through alliances) that he did not want religious coercion:

> When you meet your enemies who are polytheists, invite them to three courses of action. If they respond to any one of these, you must accept it and withhold yourself from doing them any harm. Invite them to accept

Islam; if they respond to you, accept it from them and do not fight them. ... If they refuse to accept Islam but keep their own religion, demand from them the Jizya. If they agree to pay it, accept it from them and do not put your hands on them. Only if they refuse to pay the tax, seek Allah's help and fight them.[323]

Moreover, even in the aforementioned case of the Banu al-Harith ibn Ka'b, which seemed to involve a threat of armed force to impose Islam, the sources reveal that the diplomatic coercion applied was unusually heavy for a unique reason. It was because this clan had a fierce reputation for aggressive resistance ("whenever you were driven away, you pushed to return") and conquest ("defeating those you fought"), something Muhammad mentioned to them when they sent a delegation to him.[324]

Thus, we see Muhammad the diplomat as a leader of remarkable aptitude and accomplishment, steadily increasing his polity's political strength through treaties and pledges of loyalty. At various times he used persuasion, compromise and coercion, carefully choosing was what needed in the particular circumstances.

Conclusion

Historian and theorist Martin van Creveld once described Napoleon Bonaparte as "the most competent human being who ever lived".[325] He identified Napoleon as possessing a rare combination of will, intellect, and mental and physical energy, and attributed to him almost unparalleled success as a social, political and military leader. Napoleon was not, however, a religious man, let alone a religious leader, and his undeniable brilliance never found expression in new or influential ideas on morality or spirituality. In that sense, he somehow seems less complete or rounded than Muhammad, an equally uncommon man with a combination of gifts also found in very few leaders, but who gave the world a new set of ideas on how humans should relate to God and interact with each other that has survived for 1,400 years.

The task in this short book was not to say how "competent" Muhammad was, to use van Creveld's phrase, or to analyse his contribution to history. It was not even to say what type of man he was. Far more modestly, the task was only to investigate what the early Arabic sources reveal about his capacity and aptitude for leadership and to make a determination whether and to what degree he acted in ways that produced positive results, especially those he actually sought, during his twenty-three years as a leader.

Those sources clearly show that Muhammad managed to achieve truly remarkable outcomes. After a decade of struggle within a hostile population of his fellow townsfolk in Mecca, he managed to transform Arabia within ten years of arriving in

Medina as an arbiter, *and an outsider*, in 622 CE. He made the most of this opportunity, choosing not to serve merely as a mediator in the squabbles between Medina's tribes, but to advance a far grander vision for himself and also, and *especially*, for the people around him. His vision did not grow from a desire to acquire and use power, but, rather, to create a movement of religious reform that emphasised strict monotheism and moral behaviour in conformity with what God revealed to and through him. But to spread this movement, and nurture its growth beyond infancy so that it would survive after his own death, he would need to acquire at least some power, a reality that he grasped very early on.

His ability to see and exploit opportunities, and his profound and intuitive understanding of human nature, allowed him to consolidate and expand power at an unimagined pace. Thus, by the time of his death in 632 he had effectively gained the submission of much of Arabia and created the framework of *Sunna*, meaning the example of how he had done things, that his successors ostensibly used as their model when they spread out of Arabia onto the world stage.

Muhammad understood authority, both in its strict forms (after all, he lived in a distinctly brutal environment) and in its nuanced and sensitively applied forms. His distaste of the former and desire to make the latter the norm, which he worked hard to accomplish, made him not only a leader to obey, the same as the other tribal leaders, but also one to respect, love and emulate.

Committed to getting the most from the Arab tradition of Shura, "consultation," he steadfastly involved as many trusted people as he considered practicable in his major decisions. He liked participation and consensus, and saw the benefits they brought in terms of enhanced commitment. Yet he also took some decisions contrary to the majority or the consensus, demonstrating significant moral courage, when his sense of certainty demanded such decisiveness.

He also recognised that the goals he had were new, untried, audacious, and stunningly grandiose, and that he could only achieve them if he brought everyone on the same journey. He therefore worked tirelessly to teach and persuade his followers that his vision would be beneficial for them as individuals, as a community, and as members of what would become a larger human family. Aware of human nature and concerns for comfort and wellbeing, he eschewed ascetic ideas in favour of a more appealing message: that submission to God's laws, devotion to prayer and charity, and common goodness to each other, would be rewarded in this world and the next.

Using weekly and intermittent sermons as well as other speeches and individual conversations, he communicated his vision with startling clarity, repetitively using a small number of nuanced and powerful motifs to highlight the key elements of this vision and the steps that followers would need to take to build the world he envisaged. Spellbinding when revealing God's words and equally convincing with his own, he spoke with such sincerity, certainty and precision, repeating his key points, that his followers were both convinced of their truth and able to remember them vividly.

Religious leaders are unlike other leaders. Rational considerations of ends, means and ways are far less important than the belief that God has limitless power and is capable of creating change or delivering outcomes that other leaders would consider impossible. Muhammad believed that, as a divinely assigned prophet, he could even pursue goals that today seem beyond any one man's grasp. This certainty that God was on his side — or more accurately, that he was on God's side — also allowed him to mount a courageous, spirited and effective response to vastly greater enemy forces in most of the large battles he fought, including those of Badr, Uhud and the Trench.

Yet in terms of each of the sequential steps to be taken in pursuit of those goals, he did keep his mind firmly on practicalities and feasibility. He was, after all, the practical man who corrected a Bedouin who had left his camel untied and able to wander. He asked Muhammad whether he should tie it or trust God to stop it walking off. Muhammad replied: "Tie it, *and* put your trust in Allah."[326] In other words, even faith did not absolve responsibility to plan sensibly and take care of what was necessary in practical terms. Muhammad therefore worked hard on developing plans and acquiring and apportioning resources. At each stage of his unfolding strategy he carefully planned the actions he needed to take to reach the following stage. He had a gift for planning sequences of activities that would, one-by-one, deliver him what he wanted.

Understanding that followership is strongest when the leader is seen to be sharing the same privations, hardships, risks and dangers as his followers, Muhammad exhausted himself physically among his people, ate what they ate, journeyed how they did, slept rough while on campaigns, and fought in their midst. He shared the same risk that at any moment his life, committed into God's hands in fervent prayers, could be extinguished. Seeing this, his followers sometimes even sacrificed themselves to ensure his survival.

His remarkable bond with his people was greatly aided by his common touch; his ability to simultaneously project himself credibly as the Prophet of God but yet as an ordinary man who could relate and appeal to those from all walks of life, including the poor and the powerless. People wanted to follow him because, although they knew he was a prophet and leader, with higher moral conduct, he never adopted an air of superiority but seemed in many ways to be similar to them with ordinary tastes, interests and enjoyments.

He chose his advisors and key supporters with care and insight, and ensured that everyone else would have access to him if they were close and be exposed to his ideas and expectations if they were further away. He delegated easily and often, routinely using a simple pattern of four consecutive phases: selecting, training, trusting, and rewarding the right people. He was a clever talent-spotter and, after preparing individuals through his or another senior figure's informal but thorough mentoring, assigned ever larger and more complex tasks to the people in whom he saw potential.

When he did empower people to undertake certain tasks or responsibilities, he tried hard to remove needless constraints, leaving them with some freedom for initiative and judgment. Believing that it was better to make mistakes in forgiveness than to make them in punishment, he was gentle with people and tolerant of mistakes, never rebuking anyone for lack of success if they had done their best. Believing that many humans are frail, foolish and disobedient by nature, with not even a prophet in their midst being enough to transform them, at least quickly, he was also remarkably forgiving when disobeyed. This did occasionally happen and it hurt him, but he always moved swiftly to rebuild goodwill and harmony. He believed in rewarding excellence or special effort, and, in an age well before medals and honours lists emerged, used a variety of ways — including the giving of gifts and public recognition — to express his appreciation and see that people who had done well felt rewarded.

It has thus become clear that the early Arabic sources for Muhammad's life are sufficient in their breadth, depth and consistency to reconstruct a picture of his leadership that explains its great success. He was a leader of the first order, with unusually high levels of aptitude, intuition, talent and capacity. He was also self-reflective about the way he undertook matters, learning quickly how to do something better each time and making mental notes of what worked or did not, so that he could embrace what succeeded and avoid what failed. Muhammad was a profoundly effective leader.

Postscript:
Lessons for Leaders

Historians ordinarily stick to the past, not seeing their work as having or needing a practical or normative function. They hope that their reconstruction of the past will be interesting and illuminating in and of itself, revealing observations and insights about the human condition that might cause deeper thinking about whether any "meaning" should be sought or could be gained. They usually do not write with the intention to make their work "useful"; this is, able to be used by readers for any practical purposes.

As a scholar from a so-called developed country who lives in the twenty-first century within a society governed by the rule of law and concepts of freedom and individualism, I am acutely aware of the fallacy of trying to relate the events of seventh-century Arabia to today. There are almost no continuities or similarities. The Arabia that Muhammad was born into may have been as wild, brutal and violent as most of the Christian countries of that time, but fourteen hundred years have passed and today's world is very different.

The dominating features of seventh-century Arabia, the cradle of Islam, included tribalism, blood feuds, continuous competition for resources, wealth and prestige between small communities, few laws applicable to all, and no overarching government that might create and maintain any type of wider order. Significant progress has occurred and those features are no longer present in most places in today's world.

Muhammad's desire to change Arabia and the wider world

does not remove the fact that the only way a historian can really make sense of Muhammad's leadership practices and techniques is to see them within, and existing as a consequence of, their unique historical context. Removing them from that context creates significant intellectual challenges. Any attempt to say whether there is anything enduring, universal (that, is, non-contextual) and useful in terms of "lessons" must rest upon a degree of certainty that the nature of the human experience is somehow unchanged. One must be bold enough to assert that "what worked then will still work today".

I would not assert this, at least without framing the opinion with large caveats, but it is clear that human nature — the characteristics, motivations and behaviors that seem common to all people, including innate ways of thinking, feeling, and acting — has remained fairly constant. The complex social interactions and factors that made humans envious, angry, fearful, satisfied, dedicated and loyal during seventh century Arabia still have those effects today.

It is also clear Muhammad had a natural, deep and correct appreciation of human psychology and knew how to inspire and motivate people. He demonstrated leadership behavior, and employed certain notions and techniques, upon which today's leaders could at least reflect. After all, his leadership proved profoundly successful, changing Arabia within his lifetime and creating a corpus of *Sunnah*, behavioral examples, that 1.8 billion Muslims, a quarter of the world, still fastidiously and zealously emulate.

I study leadership and leaders, and have researched and published on both. I have also had the honour of spending more than two decades teaching it to military and civilian leaders in several countries. If a student were to ask me whether Muhammad was an effective leader I would reply without hesitation in the affirmative: yes, he was a highly gifted man and an extraordinary leader. If they pressed me further, wanting me to strip away the historical context of Muhammad's Arabia to see whether we might be able to identify from his fascinating life any enduring "lessons" of how a leader might want to consider doing things today, I would write them a list much like the one I offer here:

꙳ Character and qualities
- Personify and exemplify the best human qualities and values
- Do not be seen as ambitious or status-conscious
- Never adopt an air of superiority
- Avoid any self-interest or even the appearance of it
- Be humble, flexible and open to learning from others
- Continuously self-reflect
- Do not keep doing what does not work
- Learn quickly from mistakes

꙳ Strategic Vision
- Develop a vision for creating a better situation
- If your vision is bold, be prepared for resistance
- Persevere and don't surrender that vision
- Turn that vision into a meaningful set of goals
- Create the sequence of steps needed to achieve them
- Resource each of those sufficiently

꙳ Strategic Communication
- Explain your vision to everyone who will play a role or be affected
- Explain it frequently using a few carefully chosen key motifs
- Be knowledgeable and assured to establish your credibility
- But also be modest, steady and calm
- Explain clearly why the vision matters and how it will improve things
- Explain clearly how your people will benefit
- Explain clearly what you need them to accomplish
- Remember to appeal to both the intellect and emotions

❧ Consensus Building
- Identify any factions or potentially competing interests and needs among you people
- Try to find cooperative solutions that will meet all parties' interests and needs
- Keep watching to ensure as you proceed that everyone can live with the likely outcome
- Ensure that everyone will benefit
- Ensure that everyone *knows* that they will benefit

❧ Learning from Others
- Consult others often and with an open mind and genuine desire for the critique of your ideas
- Consult people who know what they are talking about and have proven themselves trustworthy
- Do it in a group setting, not just privately with individuals
- Create an environment in which everyone knows they can approach you with ideas
- If anyone has better ideas or plans than yours do not become defensive
- Try to establish what the majority view is and, if it is likely to move the team forward towards the goals, act upon it
- If it is less likely to do so than your own idea would, have the moral courage to explain why you will not be adopting their view on that occasion
- Give credit and praise to the person whose idea or plan you use

❧ Establishing Rapport
- Learn about your people's interests, hopes and anxieties
- Search for common ground
- Share in every difficulty that you ask your people to endure
- Work as hard as your most energetic team members
- Be empathetic

- Genuinely listen and do not interrupt or talk over anyone

❧ Choosing the Right Way of Dealing with any Opposition
- Rely on persuasion, not power
- Be prepared to compromise or surrender short-term goals if doing so will bring longer-terms benefits or if the opposition at any time becomes too great
- Be prepared to apply reasonable and suitable pressure if anyone cannot be persuaded or will not compromise

❧ Managing People
- Select the right people by looking for intelligence, passion, energy and reliability
- Do this even if you do not especially like them
- Never show anyone that you do not like them
- Train them as fully as you can through example
- Trust them to undertake increasingly difficult tasks
- Tell them *what* you want, and *why*, but not *how* they should do it
- Reward them for accomplishment
- Let a person's success with one responsibility be the basis for receiving a larger responsibility
- Always praise in public
- Overlook imperfections
- Forgive failure if a person has done their best
- Never accept immorality

Chronology

570	Muhammad was born in Mecca
610	Muhammad received the first divine revelation
613	Muhammad began his public ministry
622	The Hijra: Muhammad emigrated to Medina
624	(March) Battle of Badr
625	(March) Battle of Uhud
627	(March-April) Battle of the Trench
628	(March) Treaty of Hudaybiyyah
628	(April) Conquest of Khaybar
629	Battle of Mu'tah
630	(January) Liberation of Mecca
630	(February) Battle of Hunayn
630	(February-March) Battle of Ta'if
630	(October) March to Tabuk
632	Muhammad died in Medina

Glossary

Ahadith	"Reports" or "traditions"; the recorded sayings and practices of Muhammad
Al-Waqidi	Muhammad ibn 'Umar-al-Waqidi, author of *Kitab al-Maghazi,* an early history of Muhammad's campaigns
Allah	God in Arabic; the divine intelligence worshipped by Muslims
Ansar	Medinan citizens who took into their homes Muhammad and many followers (the Muhajirun) when they emigrated from Mecca in 622.
Ayah	The Holy Qur'an has over 6,000 verses, each of which is called an ayah
Bay'a	A formal pledge of allegiance and obedience
CE	Common Era; corresponds to the Christian dating system commonly called AD
Din	Way of life or religion
Fiqh	Islamic jurisprudence
Hadith	A written record of an oral transmission of a saying or practice attributed to Muhammad

Ibn Hisham	Abu Muhammad 'Abd al-Malik ibn Hisham ibn Ayyub al-Himyari, author of *Al-Sirah al-Nabawiyyah*, an early biography of Muhammad that is actually a recension of an earlier, now-lost work by Ibn Ishaq
Ghatafan	A powerful tribe that lived to the northeast of Medina
Quraysh	The most powerful tribe in Mecca; Muhammad's most implacable foe from 610 to 630 CE
Qur'an	Islam's holy scriptures
Ka'ba	The sacred shrine in Mecca's center
Khums	The one-fifth of the spoils of war that was Muhammad's to use and distribute
Muhajirun	Meccan Muslims who emigrated to Abyssinia but also (and especially) to Medina
Sadaqah	Charity
Shura	Consultation; can denote either a consultative body or the process of seeking consultation
Sirah	The Islamic biographies of Muhammad
Surah	The Qur'an has 114 chapters, each of which is called a surah
Surah al-Tawba	The ninth and most martial chapter of the Qur'an
Umma	Community
'Umrah	The "lesser" pilgrimage to Mecca
Zakat	The obligatory charity tax that every Muslim must pay

Endnotes

1. Robert G. Hoyland, Seeing Islam as Others Saw It: *A Survey of Christian, Jewish and Zoroastrian Writings on Early Islam* (Piscataway, NJ: Gorgias Press, 2019 edition).

2. "Diodorus Siculus: the Manuscripts of the "Bibliotheca Historica". Online at: http://www.tertullian.org/rpearse/manuscripts/diodorus_sicilus.htm

3. Rafik Issa Beekun and Jamal A. Badawi, *Leadership: An Islamic Perspective* (Maryland: Amana, 1999); Nabeel Al-Azami, *Muhammad : 11 Leadership Qualities That Changed the World* (Swansea: Claritas Books, 2019); John Adair, *The Leadership of Muhammad* (London: Kogan Page, 2010).

4. Abu Muhammad 'Abd al-Malik ibn Hisham ibn Ayyub al-Himyari, *Al-Sirah al-Nabawiyyah* (Beirut: Maktaba Allassrya, 2012); Muhammad ibn 'Umar-al-Waqidi, *Kitab al-Maghazi* (Beirut: Muassassat al-'Alami, 1989); Muhammad ibn Sa'd ibn Mani' al-Hashim, *Kitab al-Tabaqat al-Kabir* (Kitab Bhavan, 2009 ed.).

5. *Sunan Abu Dawud* (Riyadh: Dar al-Haddarah lil-Nasha wa al-Tawziyyah, 2015), p. 375, hadith 2928:

حَدَّثَنَا عَبْدُ اللَّهِ بْنُ مَسْلَمَةَ، عَنْ مَالِكٍ، عَنْ عَبْدِ اللَّهِ بْنِ دِينَارٍ، عَنْ عَبْدِ اللَّهِ بْنِ عُمَرَ، أَنَّ رَسُولَ اللَّهِ صلى الله عليه وسلم قَالَ "أَلاَ كُلُّكُمْ رَاعٍ وَكُلُّكُمْ مَسْئُولٌ عَنْ رَعِيَّتِهِ فَالأَمِيرُ الَّذِي عَلَى النَّاسِ رَاعٍ عَلَيْهِمْ وَهُوَ مَسْئُولٌ عَنْهُمْ وَالرَّجُلُ رَاعٍ عَلَى أَهْلِ بَيْتِهِ وَهُوَ مَسْئُولٌ عَنْهُمْ وَالْمَرْأَةُ رَاعِيَةٌ عَلَى بَيْتِ بَعْلِهَا وَوَلَدِهِ وَهِيَ مَسْئُولَةٌ عَنْهُمْ وَالْعَبْدُ رَاعٍ عَلَى مَالِ سَيِّدِهِ وَهُوَ مَسْئُولٌ عَنْهُ فَكُلُّكُمْ رَاعٍ وَكُلُّكُمْ مَسْئُولٌ عَنْ رَعِيَّتِهِ".

Almost identical variants exist in other hadith collections, including *Sahih Muslim* (Cairo: Dar Al-Ghad Al-Gadid, 2007),

p. 676, hadith 1829:

حَدَّثَنَا قُتَيْبَةُ بْنُ سَعِيدٍ، حَدَّثَنَا لَيْثٌ، ح وَحَدَّثَنَا مُحَمَّدُ بْنُ رُمْحٍ، حَدَّثَنَا اللَّيْثُ، عَنْ نَافِعٍ، عَنِ ابْنِ عُمَرَ، عَنِ النَّبِيِّ صلى الله عليه وسلم أَنَّهُ قَالَ "أَلاَ كُلُّكُمْ رَاعٍ وَكُلُّكُمْ مَسْئُولٌ عَنْ رَعِيَّتِهِ فَالأَمِيرُ الَّذِي عَلَى النَّاسِ رَاعٍ وَهُوَ مَسْئُولٌ عَنْ رَعِيَّتِهِ وَالرَّجُلُ رَاعٍ عَلَى أَهْلِ بَيْتِهِ وَهُوَ مَسْئُولٌ عَنْهُمْ وَالْمَرْأَةُ رَاعِيَةٌ عَلَى بَيْتِ بَعْلِهَا وَوَلَدِهِ وَهِيَ مَسْئُولَةٌ عَنْهُمْ وَالْعَبْدُ رَاعٍ عَلَى مَالِ سَيِّدِهِ وَهُوَ مَسْئُولٌ عَنْهُ أَلاَ فَكُلُّكُمْ رَاعٍ وَكُلُّكُمْ مَسْئُولٌ عَنْ رَعِيَّتِهِ".

See also *Jami' al-Tirmidhi* (Beirut: Dar al-Kutub al-Ilmiyah, 2008), Vol. 2, p. 419, hadith 1705:

حَدَّثَنَا قُتَيْبَةُ، حَدَّثَنَا اللَّيْثُ، عَنْ نَافِعٍ، عَنِ ابْنِ عُمَرَ، عَنِ النَّبِيِّ صلى الله عليه وسلم قَالَ "أَلاَ كُلُّكُمْ رَاعٍ وَكُلُّكُمْ مَسْئُولٌ عَنْ رَعِيَّتِهِ فَالأَمِيرُ الَّذِي عَلَى النَّاسِ رَاعٍ وَمَسْئُولٌ عَنْ رَعِيَّتِهِ وَالرَّجُلُ رَاعٍ عَلَى أَهْلِ بَيْتِهِ وَهُوَ مَسْئُولٌ عَنْهُمْ وَالْمَرْأَةُ رَاعِيَةٌ عَلَى بَيْتِ بَعْلِهَا وَهِيَ مَسْئُولَةٌ عَنْهُ وَالْعَبْدُ رَاعٍ عَلَى مَالِ سَيِّدِهِ وَهُوَ مَسْئُولٌ عَنْهُ أَلاَ فَكُلُّكُمْ رَاعٍ وَكُلُّكُمْ مَسْئُولٌ عَنْ رَعِيَّتِهِ". قَالَ أَبُو عِيسَى وَفِي الْبَابِ عَنْ أَبِي هُرَيْرَةَ وَأَنَسٍ وَأَبِي مُوسَى. وَحَدِيثُ أَبِي مُوسَى غَيْرُ مَحْفُوظٍ وَحَدِيثُ أَنَسٍ غَيْرُ مَحْفُوظٍ وَحَدِيثُ ابْنِ عُمَرَ حَدِيثٌ حَسَنٌ صَحِيحٌ.

6   *Surah al-Isra* 17.34.

7   *Surah al-Isra* 17.36.

8   *Al-Adab Al-Mufrad* (Beirut: Dar Al-Kotob Al-Ilmiyah, 2004), p. 306:

حَدَّثَنَا عَمْرُو بْنُ خَالِدٍ، قَالَ: حَدَّثَنَا بَكْرٌ، عَنِ ابْنِ عَجْلاَنَ، أَنَّ وَهْبَ بْنَ كَيْسَانَ أَخْبَرَهُ، وَكَانَ وَهْبٌ أَدْرَكَ عَبْدَ اللَّهِ بْنَ عُمَرَ، أَنَّ ابْنَ عُمَرَ رَأَى رَاعِيًا وَغَنَمًا فِي مَكَانٍ قَبِيحٍ وَرَأَى مَكَانًا أَمْثَلَ مِنْهُ، فَقَالَ لَهُ: وَيْحَكَ، يَا رَاعِي، حَوِّلْهَا، فَإِنِّي سَمِعْتُ رَسُولَ اللَّهِ صلى الله عليه وسلم يَقُولُ: كُلُّ رَاعٍ مَسْئُولٌ عَنْ رَعِيَّتِهِ.

9   *Sahih al-Bukhari* (Cairo: Dar Al-Afaq al-Arabia, 2004), pp. 686-687, hadith 3406:

حَدَّثَنَا يَحْيَى بْنُ بُكَيْرٍ، حَدَّثَنَا اللَّيْثُ، عَنْ يُونُسَ، عَنِ ابْنِ شِهَابٍ، عَنْ أَبِي سَلَمَةَ بْنِ عَبْدِ الرَّحْمَنِ، أَنَّ جَابِرَ بْنَ عَبْدِ اللَّهِ رضى الله عنهما ـ قَالَ كُنَّا مَعَ رَسُولِ اللَّهِ صلى الله عليه وسلم نَجْنِي الْكَبَاثَ، وَإِنَّ رَسُولَ اللَّهِ صلى الله عليه وسلم قَالَ "عَلَيْكُمْ بِالأَسْوَدِ مِنْهُ، فَإِنَّهُ أَطْيَبُهُ". قَالُوا أَكُنْتَ تَرْعَى الْغَنَمَ؟ قَالَ "وَهَلْ مِنْ نَبِيٍّ إِلاَّ وَقَدْ رَعَاهَا".

10 *Al-Adab Al-Mufrad*, p. 404:

حَدَّثَنَا مُحَمَّدُ بْنُ بَشَّارٍ، قَالَ: حَدَّثَنَا مُحَمَّدُ بْنُ جَعْفَرٍ، قَالَ: حَدَّثَنَا شُعْبَةُ، سَمِعْتُ أَبَا إِسْحَاقَ، سَمِعْتُ عَبْدَةَ بْنَ حَزْنٍ يَقُولُ: تَفَاخَرَ أَهْلُ الإِبِلِ وَأَصْحَابُ الشَّاءِ، فَقَالَ النَّبِيُّ صلى الله عليه وسلم: بُعِثَّ مُوسَى وَهُوَ رَاعِي غَنَمٍ، وَبُعِثَ دَاوُدُ وَهُوَ رَاعٍ، وَبُعِثْتُ أَنَا وَأَنَا أَرْعَى غَنَمًا لأَهْلِي بِأَجْيَادٍ.

11 *Sahih al Bukhari*, p. 439, hadith 2262:

حَدَّثَنَا أَحْمَدُ بْنُ مُحَمَّدٍ الْمَكِّيُّ، حَدَّثَنَا عَمْرُو بْنُ يَحْيَى، عَنْ جَدِّهِ، عَنْ أَبِي هُرَيْرَةَ رضى الله عنه عَنِ النَّبِيِّ صلى الله عليه وسلم قَالَ "مَا بَعَثَ اللَّهُ نَبِيًّا إِلاَّ رَعَى الْغَنَمَ". فَقَالَ أَصْحَابُهُ وَأَنْتَ؟ فَقَالَ: "نَعَمْ كُنْتُ أَرْعَاهَا عَلَى قَرَارِيطَ لأَهْلِ مَكَّةَ".

12 *Sahih al-Bukhari*, p. 662, hadith 3301:

حَدَّثَنَا عَبْدُ اللَّهِ بْنُ يُوسُفَ، أَخْبَرَنَا مَالِكٌ، عَنْ أَبِي الزِّنَادِ، عَنِ الأَعْرَجِ، عَنْ أَبِي هُرَيْرَةَ ـ رضى الله عنه ـ أَنَّ رَسُولَ اللَّهِ صلى الله عليه وسلم قَالَ "رَأْسُ الْكُفْرِ نَحْوَ الْمَشْرِقِ، وَالْفَخْرُ وَالْخُيَلاَءُ فِي أَهْلِ الْخَيْلِ وَالإِبِلِ، وَالْفَدَّادِينَ أَهْلِ الْوَبَرِ، وَالسَّكِينَةُ فِي أَهْلِ الْغَنَمِ".

13 Parvaneh Pourshariati, *Decline and Fall of the Sasanian Empire: The Sasanian-Parthian Confederacy and the Arab Conquest of Iran* (London: I. B. Taurus, 2008), p. 207.

14 *Sunan al-Nasa'i* (Riyadh: Darussalam, 1999) p. 730, hadith 5390:

أَخْبَرَنَا مُحَمَّدُ بْنُ الْمُثَنَّى، قَالَ حَدَّثَنَا خَالِدُ بْنُ الْحَارِثِ، قَالَ حَدَّثَنَا حُمَيْدٌ، عَنِ الْحَسَنِ، عَنْ أَبِي بَكْرَةَ، قَالَ عَصَمَنِي اللَّهُ بِشَيْءٍ سَمِعْتُهُ مِنْ رَسُولِ اللَّهِ صلى الله عليه وسلم لَمَّا هَلَكَ كِسْرَى قَالَ "مَنِ اسْتَخْلَفُوا؟". قَالُوا بِنْتَهُ. قَالَ "لَنْ يُفْلِحَ قَوْمٌ وَلَّوْا أَمْرَهُمُ امْرَأَةً".

See also *Sahih al-Bukhari,* p. 878, hadith 4425:

حَدَّثَنَا عُثْمَانُ بْنُ الْهَيْثَمِ، حَدَّثَنَا عَوْفٌ، عَنِ الْحَسَنِ، عَنْ أَبِي بَكْرَةَ، قَالَ لَقَدْ نَفَعَنِي اللَّهُ بِكَلِمَةٍ سَمِعْتُهَا مِنْ رَسُولِ اللَّهِ صلى الله عليه وسلم أَيَّامَ الْجَمَلِ، بَعْدَ مَا كِدْتُ أَنْ أَلْحَقَ بِأَصْحَابِ الْجَمَلِ فَأُقَاتِلَ مَعَهُمْ قَالَ لَمَّا بَلَغَ رَسُولَ اللَّهِ صلى الله عليه وسلم أَنَّ أَهْلَ فَارِسَ قَدْ مَلَّكُوا عَلَيْهِمْ بِنْتَ كِسْرَى قَالَ "لَنْ يُفْلِحَ قَوْمٌ وَلَّوْا أَمْرَهُمُ امْرَأَةً".

And *Jami' al-Tirmidhi,* Vol. 4, p. 263, hadith 2262:

حَدَّثَنَا مُحَمَّدُ بْنُ الْمُثَنَّى، حَدَّثَنَا خَالِدُ بْنُ الْحَارِثِ، حَدَّثَنَا حُمَيْدٌ الطَّوِيلُ، عَنِ الْحَسَنِ، عَنْ أَبِي بَكْرَةَ، قَالَ عَصَمَنِي اللَّهُ بِشَيْءٍ سَمِعْتُهُ مِنْ رَسُولِ اللَّهِ صلى الله

عليه وسلم لَمَّا هَلَكَ كِسْرَى قَالَ "مَنِ اسْتَخْلَفُوا؟". قَالُوا ابْنَتَهُ. فَقَالَ النَّبِيُّ صلى الله عليه وسلم "لَنْ يُفْلِحَ قَوْمٌ وَلَّوْا أَمْرَهُمُ امْرَأَةً" . قَالَ فَلَمَّا قَدِمَتْ عَائِشَةُ يَعْنِي الْبَصْرَةَ ذَكَرْتُ قَوْلَ رَسُولِ اللَّهِ صلى الله عليه وسلم فَعَصَمَنِي اللَّهُ بِهِ. قَالَ أَبُو عِيسَى هَذَا حَدِيثٌ صَحِيحٌ.

15 *Surah al-Naml* 27.22-44. Amina Wadud, *Quran and Woman: Re-Reading the Sacred Text from a Woman's Perspective* (New York: Oxford University Press, 1999), pp. 29-44.

16 Jonathan A.C. Brown, *Hadith: Muhammad's Legacy in the Medieval and Modern World* (Oxford: Oneworld, 2009. 2011 edition), p. 249; Fatema Mernissi, *Women and Islam: An Historical and Theological Enquiry* Translated by Mary Jo Lakeland (Oxford: Blackwell, 1987), p. 76.

17 For the role in women during war, see Joel Hayward, *Civilian Immunity in Foundational Islamic Strategic Thought: A Historical Enquiry* (Amman: The Royal Islamic Strategic Studies Centre, 2018), esp. pp. 12-16.

18 *Surah al-Anbiyah* 21.73.

19 *Surah al-Sajdah* 32.24.

20 *Surah al-Tawbah* 9.12.

21 *Surah al-Qasas* 28.41.

22 *Surah al-Ahqaf* 46.12.

23 *Surah al-Insan* 76.24.

24 *Surah al-Nisa* 4.59.

25 *Sahih al-Bukhari*, p. 1400, hadith 4584.

26 Edward William Lane, *An Arabic-English Lexicon Derived from the Best and Most Copious Eastern Sources* (London: Willams & Norgate 1863), Vol. 1, pp. 95-97.

27 *Surah al-Nisa* 4.64.

28 *Surah Al-Imran* 3.50.

29 Κατὰ Ἰωάννην (Book of John) 14.15 and Κατὰ Λουκᾶν

(Luke) 6.46, *KATA IΩANNHNKATA IΩANNHNKATA IΩANNHNNovum Testamentum Graece.*

30   דברים תורה הרות נביאים וכתובים 18.18-19

31   *Surah al-Nisa* 4.80.

32   *Sahih al-Bukhari*, p. 1400, hadith 7137:

حَدَّثَنَا عَبْدَانُ، أَخْبَرَنَا عَبْدُ اللَّهِ، عَنْ يُونُسَ، عَنِ الزُّهْرِيِّ، أَخْبَرَنِي أَبُو سَلَمَةَ بْنُ عَبْدِ الرَّحْمَنِ، أَنَّهُ سَمِعَ أَبَا هُرَيْرَةَ ـ رضى الله عنه ـ أَنَّ رَسُولَ اللَّهِ صلى الله عليه وسلم قَالَ " مَنْ أَطَاعَنِي فَقَدْ أَطَاعَ اللَّهَ، وَمَنْ عَصَانِي فَقَدْ عَصَى اللَّهَ، وَمَنْ أَطَاعَ أَمِيرِي فَقَدْ أَطَاعَنِي، وَمَنْ عَصَى أَمِيرِي فَقَدْ عَصَانِي".

Strikingly similar variants of this hadith are found in all the *Kutub al-Sittah*, the six canonical Sunni ahadith collections.

33   *Surah al-Nisa* 4.14.

34   Ibn Hisham, *Al-Sirah al-Nabawiyyah*, p. 457.

35   *Surah al-Imran* 3.152.

36   *Surah al-Imran* 3.159.

37   Ella Landau-Tasseron, *The Religious Foundations of Political Allegiance: A Study of Bay'a in Pre-modern Islam* Research Monographs on the Muslim World, Series No 2, Paper No 4, May, 2010 (Washington DC: Hudson Institute).

38   *Surah al-Fath* 48.10.

39   Landau-Tasseron, pp. 5-6.

40   *Sahih al-Bukhari*, p. 1400, hadith 7202:

حَدَّثَنَا عَبْدُ اللَّهِ بْنُ يُوسُفَ، أَخْبَرَنَا مَالِكٌ، عَنْ عَبْدِ اللَّهِ بْنِ دِينَارٍ، عَنْ عَبْدِ اللَّهِ بْنِ عُمَرَ ـ رضى الله عنهما ـ قَالَ كُنَّا إِذَا بَايَعْنَا رَسُولَ اللَّهِ صلى الله عليه وسلم عَلَى السَّمْعِ وَالطَّاعَةِ يَقُولُ لَنَا "فِيمَا اسْتَطَعْتَ".

See also: *Sahih al-Bukhari*, p. 144, hadith 7204; *Sahih Muslim*, p. 690, hadith 1867; *Sunan Ibn Majah* (Cairo: Dar al-Hadith, 2005), Vol. 2, p. 537, hadith 2868; *Sunan al-Nasa'i*, p. 582, hadith 4179.

41   Ibn Hisham, *Al-Sirah al-Nabawiyyah*, p. 821.

42 Cf. *Sunan Abu Dawud*, p. 332, hadith 2626.

43 Cf. *Sunan Abu Dawud*, p. 332, hadith 2626.

44 *Sunan al-Nasa'i*, p. 581, hadith 4168.

45 *Sunan Abu Dawud*, p. 332, hadith 2625.

46 *Sahih al-Bukhari*, p. 1401, hadith 7145:

حَدَّثَنَا عُمَرُ بْنُ حَفْصِ بْنِ غِيَاثٍ، حَدَّثَنَا أَبِي، حَدَّثَنَا الأَعْمَشُ، حَدَّثَنَا سَعْدُ بْنُ عُبَيْدَةَ، عَنْ أَبِي عَبْدِ الرَّحْمَنِ، عَنْ عَلِيٍّ ـ رضى الله عنه ـ قَالَ بَعَثَ النَّبِيُّ صلى الله عليه وسلم سَرِيَّةً، وَأَمَّرَ عَلَيْهِمْ رَجُلاً مِنَ الأَنْصَارِ وَأَمَرَهُمْ أَنْ يُطِيعُوهُ، فَغَضِبَ عَلَيْهِمْ وَقَالَ أَلَيْسَ قَدْ أَمَرَ النَّبِيُّ صلى الله عليه وسلم أَنْ تُطِيعُونِي قَالُوا بَلَى. قَالَ عَزَمْتُ عَلَيْكُمْ لَمَا جَمَعْتُمْ حَطَبًا وَأَوْقَدْتُمْ نَارًا، ثُمَّ دَخَلْتُمْ فِيهَا، فَجَمَعُوا حَطَبًا فَأَوْقَدُوا، فَلَمَّا هَمُّوا بِالدُّخُولِ فَقَامَ يَنْظُرُ بَعْضُهُمْ إِلَى بَعْضٍ، قَالَ بَعْضُهُمْ إِنَّمَا تَبِعْنَا النَّبِيَّ صلى الله عليه وسلم فِرَارًا مِنَ النَّارِ، أَفَنَدْخُلُهَا، فَبَيْنَمَا هُمْ كَذَلِكَ إِذْ خَمَدَتِ النَّارُ، وَسَكَنَ غَضَبُهُ، فَذُكِرَ لِلنَّبِيِّ صلى الله عليه وسلم فَقَالَ " لَوْ دَخَلُوهَا مَا خَرَجُوا مِنْهَا أَبَدًا، إِنَّمَا الطَّاعَةُ فِي الْمَعْرُوفِ ".

Cf. *Sahih Muslim*, p. 681, hadith 1840b.

47 *Surah al-Fath* 48.10.

48 Fred Donner, *The Early Islamic Conquests* (Princeton University Press, 1981), p. 67.

49 *Surah al-Fath* 48.18, 19.

50 Muhammad Nazeer Ka Ka Khel, "The Conceptual and Institutional Development of Shura in Early Islam", *Islamic Studies*, Vol. 19, No. 4 (Winter 1980), pp. 271-282.

51 *Surah al-Shura* 42.38.

52 *Sunan Ibn Majah*, Vol. 2, p. 325, hadith 2318; *Sahih al-Bukhari*, p. 1406, hadith 7169; *Sahih Muslim*, p. 928, hadith 2601a; *Sunan Abu Dawud*, p. 452, hadith 3583; *Sunan al-Nasa'i*, pp. 737-738, hadith 5424; et. al.

53 Al-Waqidi, *Kitab al-Maghazi*, Vol. 1, p. 48.

54 Ibid, p. 53.

55 Ibid.

56	Vol 3, p. 925.
57	*Surah al-Najm* 53.3, 4.
58	Al-Waqidi, *Kitab al-Maghazi*, Vol. 3, p. 937; Ibn Sa'd, *Kitab al-Tabaqat al-Kabir*, Vol. 2, p. 196.
59	*Sahih al-Bukhari*, pp. 1212, 1463, hadiths 6086, 7480.
60	*Sunan Ibn Majah*, Vol. 1, pp. 289-290, hadith 706.
61	*Sunan Abu Dawud*, p. 69, hadith 498.
62	*Sunan Ibn Majah*, Vol. 1, p. 290, hadith 707.
63	*Sunan Abu Dawud*, p. 635, hadith 5128.
64	*Sahih al-Bukhari*, p. 1432, hadith 7307.
65	Al-Waqidi, *Kitab al-Maghazi*, Vol. 1, p. 56.
66	Ibid., Vol. 2, p. 445.
67	Ibid., Vol. 1, pp. 208-2011.
68	Ibid., Vol. 2, p. 445.
69	Ibn Sa'd, *Kitab al-Tabaqat al-Kabir*, Vol. 2, p. 81.
70	Ibn Hisham, *Al-Sirah al-Nabawiyyah*, pp. 747-748; Al-Waqidi, *Kitab al-Maghazi*, Vol. 2, p. 610.
71	*Surah Al-Fath* 48.1
72	Al-Waqidi, *Kitab al-Maghazi*, Vol. 2, p. 617.
73	*Sahih al-Bukhari*, pp. 97, 785-786, hadiths 428, 3932.
74	Ibn Hisham, *Al-Sirah al-Nabawiyyah*, p. 337. Cf. *Sahih al-Bukhari*, pp. 779-780, hadith 3906.
75	*Surah al-Ahzab* 33.21.
76	*Sahih al-Bukhari, pp. 818-819, hadith 4101:*

حَدَّثَنَا خَلَّادُ بْنُ يَحْيَى، حَدَّثَنَا عَبْدُ الْوَاحِدِ بْنُ أَيْمَنَ، عَنْ أَبِيهِ، قَالَ أَتَيْتُ جَابِرًا ـ رضى الله عنه ـ فَقَالَ إِنَّا يَوْمَ الْخَنْدَقِ نَحْفِرُ فَعَرَضَتْ كُدْيَةٌ شَدِيدَةٌ، فَجَاءُوا النَّبِيَّ صلى الله عليه وسلم فَقَالُوا هَذِهِ كُدْيَةٌ عَرَضَتْ فِي الْخَنْدَقِ، فَقَالَ " أَنَا نَازِلٌ ". ثُمَّ قَامَ وَبَطْنُهُ مَعْصُوبٌ بِحَجَرٍ، وَلَبِثْنَا ثَلَاثَةَ أَيَّامٍ لاَ نَذُوقُ ذَوَاقًا، فَأَخَذَ النَّبِيُّ صلى

الله عليه وسلم الْمِعْوَلَ فَضَرَبَ، فَعَادَ كَثِيبًا أَهْيَلَ أَوْ أَهْيَمَ، فَقُلْتُ يَا رَسُولَ اللَّهِ ائْذَنْ لِي إِلَى الْبَيْتِ. فَقُلْتُ لِامْرَأَتِي رَأَيْتُ بِالنَّبِيِّ صلى الله عليه وسلم شَيْئًا، مَا كَانَ فِي ذَلِكَ صَبْرٌ، فَعِنْدَكِ شَيْءٌ قَالَتْ عِنْدِي شَعِيرٌ وَعَنَاقٌ. فَذَبَحْتُ الْعَنَاقَ وَطَحَنَتِ الشَّعِيرَ، حَتَّى جَعَلْنَا اللَّحْمَ فِي الْبُرْمَةِ، ثُمَّ جِئْتُ النَّبِيَّ صلى الله عليه وسلم وَالْعَجِينُ قَدِ انْكَسَرَ، وَالْبُرْمَةُ بَيْنَ الْأَثَافِيِّ قَدْ كَادَتْ أَنْ تَنْضَجَ فَقُلْتُ طُعَيِّمٌ لِي، فَقُمْ يَا رَسُولَ اللَّهِ وَرَجُلٌ أَوْ رَجُلَانِ. قَالَ " كَمْ هُوَ ". فَذَكَرْتُ لَهُ، قَالَ " كَثِيرٌ طَيِّبٌ ". قَالَ " قُلْ لَهَا لاَ تَنْزِعِ الْبُرْمَةَ وَلاَ الْخُبْزَ مِنَ التَّنُّورِ حَتَّى آتِيَ ". فَقَالَ " قُومُوا ". فَقَامَ الْمُهَاجِرُونَ وَالْأَنْصَارُ، فَلَمَّا دَخَلَ عَلَى امْرَأَتِهِ قَالَ وَيْحَكِ جَاءَ النَّبِيُّ صلى الله عليه وسلم بِالْمُهَاجِرِينَ وَالْأَنْصَارِ وَمَنْ مَعَهُمْ. قَالَتْ هَلْ سَأَلَكَ قُلْتُ نَعَمْ. فَقَالَ " ادْخُلُوا وَلاَ تَضَاغَطُوا ". فَجَعَلَ يَكْسِرُ الْخُبْزَ وَيَجْعَلُ عَلَيْهِ اللَّحْمَ، وَيُخَمِّرُ الْبُرْمَةَ وَالتَّنُّورَ إِذَا أَخَذَ مِنْهُ، وَيُقَرِّبُ إِلَى أَصْحَابِهِ ثُمَّ يَنْزِعُ، فَلَمْ يَزَلْ يَكْسِرُ الْخُبْزَ وَيَغْرِفُ حَتَّى شَبِعُوا وَبَقِيَ بَقِيَّةٌ قَالَ " كُلِي هَذَا وَأَهْدِي، فَإِنَّ النَّاسَ أَصَابَتْهُمْ مَجَاعَةٌ ".

77   Ibid. And cf. Ibn Hisham, *Al-Sirah al-Nabawiyyah*, p. 672.

78   *Sahih al-Bukhari*, pp. 594, 874-877, hadiths 2948, 4418; Al-Waqidi, *Kitab al-Maghazi*, Vol. 3, p. 998.

79   Ibid., Vol. 1, p. 24.

80   Al-Waqidi, *Kitab al-Maghazi*, Vol. 3, p. 998.

81   *Surah al-Baqarah* 2.216.

82   Al-Waqidi, *Kitab al-Maghazi*, Vol. 1, p. 67.

83   Ibn Hisham, *Al-Sirah al-Nabawiyyah*, p. 444.

84   *Sahih al-Bukhari*, pp. 588, 991, hadiths 2915, 4875, 4877; *Sahih Muslim*, p. 645, hadith 1763.

85   Ibn Hisham, *Al-Sirah al-Nabawiyyah*, p. 445.

85   Ibid., p. 445; Al-Waqidi, *Kitab al-Maghazi*, Vol. 1, p. 81.

87   Sahih al-Bukhari, p. 560, hadith 2766; *Sunan Abu Dawud*, p. 324, hadith 2536; *Sunan al-Nasa'i*, pp. 518, 560, hadiths 3701, 4009.

88   *Surah al-Anfal* 8.15, 16.

89   Ibn Hisham, *Al-Sirah al-Nabawiyyah*, pp. 572-574; Al-Waqidi, *Kitab al-Maghazi*, Vol. 1, p. 243.

90   Ibn Hisham, *Al-Sirah al-Nabawiyyah*, pp. 846-847; Al-Waqidi,

Kitab al-Maghazi, Vol. 3, pp. 899, 910; *Sahih al-Bukhari*, pp. 854, hadith 4315, 4317.

91   Al-Waqidi, *Kitab al-Maghazi*, Vol. 1, pp. 357-358.

92   Al-Waqidi, *Kitab al-Maghazi*, Vol. 1, pp. 361, 362.

93   Ibn Hisham, *Al-Sirah al-Nabawiyyah*, p. 258. The story is also found in *Sunan Abu Dawud*, p. 508, hadith 4078 and *Jami' al-Tirmidhi*, Vol. 2, p. 450, hadith 1784.

94   *Sahih Muslim*, p. 931, hadith 2609a:

حَدَّثَنَا يَحْيَى بْنُ يَحْيَى، وَعَبْدُ الأَعْلَى بْنُ حَمَّادٍ، قَالاَ كِلاَهُمَا قَرَأْتُ عَلَى مَالِكٍ عَنِ ابْنِ شِهَابٍ، عَنْ سَعِيدِ بْنِ الْمُسَيِّبِ، عَنْ أَبِي هُرَيْرَةَ، أَنَّ رَسُولَ اللَّهِ صلى الله عليه وسلم قَالَ " لَيْسَ الشَّدِيدُ بِالصُّرَعَةِ إِنَّمَا الشَّدِيدُ الَّذِي يَمْلِكُ نَفْسَهُ عِنْدَ الْغَضَبِ ".

Cf. *Sahih al-Bukhari*, p. 1218, hadith 6114 and *Sunan Abu Dawud*, p. 599, hadith 4779.

95   *Sahih al-Bukhari*, pp. 95, 579-580, 1436, hadiths 420, 2870, 7336; *Sahih Muslim*, p. 691, hadith 1870a; *Sunan Abu Dawud*, p. 328, hadith 2575; *Sunan al-Nasa'i*, p. 506, hadiths 3613, 3614.

96   *Jami' al-Tirmidhi*, Vol. 2, pp. 416-417, hadith 1699.

97   *Sahih al-Bukhari*, p. 580, hadith 2872. Cf. *Sunan al-Nasa'i*, p. 506, 507, hadiths 3618, 3622.

98   *Jami' al-Tirmidhi*, Vol. 2, p. 391, hadith 1637:

حَدَّثَنَا أَحْمَدُ بْنُ مَنِيعٍ، حَدَّثَنَا يَزِيدُ بْنُ هَارُونَ، أَخْبَرَنَا مُحَمَّدُ بْنُ إِسْحَاقَ، عَنْ عَبْدِ اللَّهِ بْنِ عَبْدِ الرَّحْمَنِ بْنِ أَبِي حُسَيْنٍ، أَنَّ رَسُولَ اللَّهِ صلى الله عليه وسلم قَالَ " إِنَّ اللَّهَ لَيُدْخِلُ بِالسَّهْمِ الْوَاحِدِ ثَلاَثَةَ الْجَنَّةَ صَانِعَهُ يَحْتَسِبُ فِي صَنْعَتِهِ الْخَيْرَ وَالرَّامِيَ بِهِ وَالْمُمِدَّ بِهِ " . وَقَالَ " ارْمُوا وَارْكَبُوا وَلأَنْ تَرْمُوا أَحَبُّ إِلَىَّ مِنْ أَنْ تَرْكَبُوا كُلُّ مَا يَلْهُو بِهِ الرَّجُلُ الْمُسْلِمُ بَاطِلٌ إِلاَّ رَمْيَهُ بِقَوْسِهِ وَتَأْدِيبَهُ فَرَسَهُ وَمُلاَعَبَتَهُ أَهْلَهُ فَإِنَّهُنَّ مِنَ الْحَقِّ ".

99   *Sunan al-Nasa'i*, p. 505, hadith 3608.

100   *Sahih Muslim*, p. 705, hadith 1917:

حَدَّثَنَا هَارُونُ بْنُ مَعْرُوفٍ، أَخْبَرَنَا ابْنُ وَهْبٍ، أَخْبَرَنِي عَمْرُو بْنُ الْحَارِثِ، عَنْ أَبِي عَلِيٍّ ثُمَامَةَ بْنِ شُفَىٍّ أَنَّهُ سَمِعَ عُقْبَةَ بْنَ عَامِرٍ، يَقُولُ سَمِعْتُ رَسُولَ اللَّهِ صلى الله عليه وسلم وَهُوَ عَلَى الْمِنْبَرِ يَقُولُ " وَأَعِدُّوا لَهُمْ مَا اسْتَطَعْتُمْ مِنْ قُوَّةٍ أَلاَ إِنَّ الْقُوَّةَ

الرَّمْىُ أَلاَ إِنَّ الْقُوَّةَ الرَّمْىُ أَلاَ إِنَّ الْقُوَّةَ الرَّمْىُ".

101   *Jami' al-Tirmidhi*, Vol. 4, p. 118, hadith 3083.

102   *Sunan Abu Dawud*, p. 327, hadith 2574:

حَدَّثَنَا أَحْمَدُ بْنُ يُونُسَ، حَدَّثَنَا ابْنُ أَبِي ذِئْبٍ، عَنْ نَافِعِ بْنِ أَبِي نَافِعٍ، عَنْ أَبِي هُرَيْرَةَ، قَالَ قَالَ رَسُولُ اللَّهِ صلى الله عليه وسلم "لاَ سَبَقَ إِلاَّ فِي خُفٍّ أَوْ فِي حَافِرٍ أَوْ نَصْلٍ".

Cf. also *Jami' al-Tirmidhi*, Vol. 2, p. 417, hadith 1700; *Sunan al-Nasa'i*, p. 506, hadiths 3615, 3616.

103   *Sahih al-Bukhari*, p. 1242, hadith 6247; *Sunan Ibn Majah*, Vol. 3, p. 307, hadith 3700.

104   *Sahih Muslim*, p. 841, hadith 2326:

وَحَدَّثَنَا أَبُو بَكْرِ بْنُ أَبِي شَيْبَةَ، حَدَّثَنَا يَزِيدُ بْنُ هَارُونَ، عَنْ حَمَّادِ بْنِ سَلَمَةَ، عَنْ ثَابِتٍ، عَنْ أَنَسٍ، أَنَّ امْرَأَةً، كَانَ فِي عَقْلِهَا شَىْءٌ فَقَالَتْ يَا رَسُولَ اللَّهِ إِنَّ لِي إِلَيْكَ حَاجَةً فَقَالَ "يَا أُمَّ فُلاَنٍ انْظُرِي أَىَّ السِّكَكِ شِئْتِ حَتَّى أَقْضِيَ لَكِ حَاجَتَكِ". فَخَلاَ مَعَهَا فِي بَعْضِ الطُّرُقِ حَتَّى فَرَغَتْ مِنْ حَاجَتِهَا.

105   *Sahih al-Bukhari*, p. 1219, hadith 6128:

حَدَّثَنَا أَبُو الْيَمَانِ، أَخْبَرَنَا شُعَيْبٌ، عَنِ الزُّهْرِيِّ، ح وَقَالَ اللَّيْثُ حَدَّثَنِي يُونُسُ، عَنِ ابْنِ شِهَابٍ، أَخْبَرَنِي عُبَيْدُ اللَّهِ بْنُ عَبْدِ اللَّهِ بْنِ عُتْبَةَ، أَنَّ أَبَا هُرَيْرَةَ، أَخْبَرَهُ أَنَّ أَعْرَابِيًّا بَالَ إِلَيْهِ النَّاسُ لِيَقَعُوا بِهِ فَقَالَ لَهُمْ رَسُولُ اللَّهِ صلى الله عليه وسلم "دَعُوهُ، وَأَهْرِيقُوا عَلَى بَوْلِهِ ذَنُوبًا مِنْ مَاءٍ ـ أَوْ سَجْلاً مِنْ مَاءٍ ـ فَإِنَّمَا بُعِثْتُمْ مُيَسِّرِينَ، وَلَمْ تُبْعَثُوا مُعَسِّرِينَ".

106   *Sunan Ibn Majah*, Vol. 1, p. 224-225, hadith 529:

حَدَّثَنَا أَبُو بَكْرِ بْنُ أَبِي شَيْبَةَ، حَدَّثَنَا عَلِيُّ بْنُ مُسْهِرٍ، عَنْ مُحَمَّدِ بْنِ عَمْرٍو، عَنْ أَبِي سَلَمَةَ، عَنْ أَبِي هُرَيْرَةَ، قَالَ دَخَلَ أَعْرَابِيٌّ الْمَسْجِدَ وَرَسُولُ اللَّهِ ـ صلى الله عليه وسلم ـ جَالِسٌ فَقَالَ اللَّهُمَّ اغْفِرْ لِي وَلِمُحَمَّدٍ وَلاَ تَغْفِرْ لأَحَدٍ مَعَنَا. فَضَحِكَ رَسُولُ اللَّهِ ـ صلى الله عليه وسلم ـ وَقَالَ "لَقَدِ احْتَظَرْتَ وَاسِعًا". ثُمَّ وَلَّى حَتَّى إِذَا كَانَ فِي نَاحِيَةِ الْمَسْجِدِ فَشَجَ يَبُولُ. فَقَالَ الأَعْرَابِيُّ بَعْدَ أَنْ فَقِهَ فَقَامَ إِلَىَّ بِأَبِي وَأُمِّي. فَلَمْ يُؤَنِّبْ وَلَمْ يَسُبَّ. فَقَالَ "إِنَّ هَذَا الْمَسْجِدَ لاَ يُبَالُ فِيهِ وَإِنَّمَا بُنِيَ لِذِكْرِ اللَّهِ وَلِلصَّلاَةِ". ثُمَّ أَمَرَ بِسَجْلٍ مِنْ مَاءٍ فَأُفْرِغَ عَلَى بَوْلِهِ.

107   *Sunan Abu Dawud*, p. 139, hadith 1109.

108   *Sunan Abu Dawud*, p. 117, hadith 918.

حَدَّثَنَا قُتَيْبَةُ، - يَعْنِي ابْنَ سَعِيدٍ - حَدَّثَنَا اللَّيْثُ، عَنْ سَعِيدِ بْنِ أَبِي سَعِيدٍ، عَنْ عَمْرِو بْنِ سُلَيْمٍ الزُّرَقِيِّ، أَنَّهُ سَمِعَ أَبَا قَتَادَةَ، يَقُولُ بَيْنَا نَحْنُ فِي الْمَسْجِدِ جُلُوسٌ خَرَجَ عَلَيْنَا رَسُولُ اللَّهِ صلى الله عليه وسلم يَحْمِلُ أُمَامَةَ بِنْتَ أَبِي الْعَاصِ بْنِ الرَّبِيعِ وَأُمُّهَا زَيْنَبُ بِنْتُ رَسُولِ اللَّهِ صلى الله عليه وسلم وَهِيَ صَبِيَّةٌ يَحْمِلُهَا عَلَى عَاتِقِهِ فَصَلَّى رَسُولُ اللَّهِ صلى الله عليه وسلم وَهِيَ عَلَى عَاتِقِهِ يَضَعُهَا إِذَا رَكَعَ وَيُعِيدُهَا إِذَا قَامَ حَتَّى قَضَى صَلَاتَهُ يَفْعَلُ ذَلِكَ بِهَا.

109 *Sahih al-Bukhari*, p. 1232, hadith 6203; *Sahih Muslim*, pp. 785-786, hadith 2150; *Sunan Ibn Majah*, Vol. 3, p. 314, hadith 3720.

110 Ibn Hisham, *Al-Sirah al-Nabawiyyah*, p. 338.

111 *Sahih al-Bukhari*, pp. 189, 1212, hadiths 948, 6081.

112 *Sahih al-Bukhari*, pp. 25-26, hadith 63.

113 *Sahih al-Bukhari*, pp. 298-299, hadith 1491:

حَدَّثَنَا آدَمُ، حَدَّثَنَا شُعْبَةُ، حَدَّثَنَا مُحَمَّدُ بْنُ زِيَادٍ، قَالَ سَمِعْتُ أَبَا هُرَيْرَةَ ـ رضى الله عنه ـ قَالَ أَخَذَ الْحَسَنُ بْنُ عَلِيٍّ ـ رضى الله عنهما ـ تَمْرَةً مِنْ تَمْرِ الصَّدَقَةِ، فَجَعَلَهَا فِي فِيهِ، فَقَالَ النَّبِيُّ صلى الله عليه وسلم " كِخْ كِخْ ـ لِيَطْرَحَهَا ثُمَّ قَالَ ـ أَمَا شَعَرْتَ أَنَّا لاَ نَأْكُلُ الصَّدَقَةَ ".

114 Ziauddin Ahmed, "Financial Policies of the Holy Prophet: A Case Study of the Distribution of Ghanima in Early Islam", *Islamic Studies*, Vol. 14, No. 1 (Spring 1975), pp. 9-25, esp. p. 10.

Cf. *Sahih al-Bukhari*, pp. 278, 617, hadiths 1395, 3072.

115 *Surah al-Anfal* 8:38.

116 *Sahih al-Bukhari*, p. 626, hadith 3117.

117 Ziauddin Ahmed, "Financial Policies", p. 11.

118 Ibid., p. 16.

119 *Sahih Muslim*, p. 642, hadith 1757a.

120 *Sahih al-Bukhari*, pp. 406, 411, 427, 496, 588, 884, hadiths 2068, 2096, 2200, 2509, 2916, 4467.

121 *Sahih al-Bukhari*, pp. 553, 587, 621, 622, 623, hadiths 2739, 2912, 3092, 3093, 3096.

122   Fred Donner, *Muhammad and the Believers at the Origins of Islam* (Cambridge, Mass, and London: Belknap Press of Harvard University Press, 2010). Donner's belief in an early Islamic ecumenism is sensible, powerfully attractive, well documented and just perhaps a little overstated.

123   Michael Lecker, *The Constitution of Medina: Muhammad's First Legal Document* (Princeton, NJ: Darwin, 2004).

124   Ibn Hisham, *Al-Sirah al-Nabawiyyah*, p. 341.

125   Ibid., p. 342.

126   *Sunan al-Nasa'i*, p. 58, hadith 432.

127   *Surah al-Anbiyah* 21.107. The word لِلْعَالَمِــينَ literally says "the worlds".

128   *Surah al-Takwir* 81.27; *Surah al-Anbiyah* 21.107. See also *Surah al-Qalam* 68.52. The word لِلْعَالَمِــينَ literally says "the worlds".

129   *Surah al-Mutaffifin* 83.6.

130   *Surah al-Anfal* 8.30.

131   *Sunan Abu Dawud*, pp. 194-195, hadith 1510:

> حَدَّثَنَا مُحَمَّدُ بْنُ كَثِيرٍ، أَخْبَرَنَا سُفْيَانُ، عَنْ عَمْرِو بْنِ مُرَّةَ، عَنْ عَبْدِ اللَّهِ بْنِ الْحَارِثِ، عَنْ طُلَيْقِ بْنِ قَيْسٍ، عَنِ ابْنِ عَبَّاسٍ، قَالَ كَانَ النَّبِيُّ صلى الله عليه وسلم يَدْعُو "رَبِّ أَعِنِّي وَلاَ تُعِنْ عَلَىَّ وَانْصُرْنِي وَلاَ تَنْصُرْ عَلَىَّ وَامْكُرْ لِي وَلاَ تَمْكُرْ عَلَىَّ وَاهْدِنِي وَيَسِّرْ هُدَاىَ إِلَىَّ وَانْصُرْنِي عَلَى مَنْ بَغَى عَلَىَّ اللَّهُمَّ اجْعَلْنِي لَكَ شَاكِرًا لَكَ ذَاكِرًا لَكَ رَاهِبًا لَكَ مِطْوَاعًا إِلَيْكَ مُخْبِتًا أَوْ مُنِيبًا رَبِّ تَقَبَّلْ تَوْبَتِي وَاغْسِلْ حَوْبَتِي وَأَجِبْ دَعْوَتِي وَثَبِّتْ حُجَّتِي وَاهْدِ قَلْبِي وَسَدِّدْ لِسَانِي وَاسْلُلْ سَخِيمَةَ قَلْبِي".

132   *Sahih al-Bukhari*, p. 615, hadith 3060.

133   *Sahih al-Bukhari*, pp. 874-877, hadith 4418; *Sahih Muslim*, pp. 980-984, hadith 2769d.

134   *Sahih al-Bukhari*, p. 300, hadith 1500.

135   Cf. Ibn Hisham, *Al-Sirah al-Nabawiyyah*, 74.

136   Al-Waqidi, *Kitab al-Maghazi*, Vol. 2, 492.

137   Ibn Hisham, *Al-Sirah al-Nabawiyyah*, 543.

138 Al-Waqidi, *Kitab al-Maghazi*, Vol. 2, 493.

139 Michael Lecker, "The Hudaybiyya-Treaty and the Expedition against Khaybar," *Jerusalem Studies in Arabic and Islam*, Vol. 5 (1984), pp. 1-11.

140 Al-Waqidi, *Kitab al-Maghazi*, Vol. 2, p. 642.

141 Ibid., Vol. 2, pp. 706-707.

142 Ibid., Vol. 2, p. 684.

143 *Sahih al-Bukhari*, p. 433, hadith 2235.

144 Donner, *The Early Islamic Conquests*, p. 64.

145 Ibn Hisham, *Al-Sirah al-Nabawiyyah*, p. 597.

146 Ahmad El-Sharif, "What can the Prophet Muhammad's Metaphors Do?" *Advances in Language and Literary Studies*, Vol. 5, No. 5 (October 2018), pp. 69-78.

147 *Sunan Ibn Majah*, Vol. 3, p. 336, hadith 3793.

148 *Sahih Muslim*, p. 682, hadith 1841.

149 *Sahih al-Bukhari*, pp. 1198, 1466, hadiths 5987, 7502; *Jami' al-Tirmidhi*, Vol. 3, p. 51, hadith 1909.

150 *Sunan Abu Dawud*, p. 608, hadith 4875.

151 *Sunan al-Nasa'i*, p. 426, hadith 3106.

152 *Sahih Muslim*, p. 700, hadith 1902.

153 *Sahih al-Bukhari*, p. 636, hadith 3158; *Sahih Muslim*, pp. 1046-1047, hadith 2961a; *Sunan Ibn Majah*, Vol. 3, p. 417, hadith 3997.

154 *Sahih al-Bukhari*, p. 1195, hadith 5971.

155 *Sahih al-Bukhari*, pp. 1053, 1164, hadiths 5146, 5767.

156 *Sahih al-Bukhari*, p. 599, hadith 2977; *Sahih Muslim*, pp. 181-182, hadiths 523a, 523b; *Sunan al-Nasa'i*, pp. 423-424, hadith 3089.

157 For the impact of Muhammad's Friday sermons on the development of Islamic ritual, liturgy and rhetoric, see Linda G. Jones, *The Power of Oratory in the Medieval Muslim World*

(Cambridge University Press, 2012).

158 *Sahih al-Bukhari*, p. 1302, hadith 6604.

159 *Sahih Muslim*, p. 705, hadith 1917.

160 *Sunan al-Nasa'i*, p. 565, hadith 4052.

161 *Sunan Abu Dawud*, p. 460, hadith 3650.

162 *Sahih al-Bukhari*, pp. 478-479, hadith 2434; *Sunan Abu Dawud*, p. 459, hadith 3649.

163 *Surah al-Jumu'ah* 62.9, 10.

164 Cf. *Sahih al-Bukhari*, pp. 823-824, hadith 4132.

165 *Sahih al-Bukhari*, p. 649, hadith 3211.

166 Ibn Sa'd, *Kitab al-Tabaqat al-Kabir*, Vol. 1, p. 440.

167 *Sahih al-Bukhari*, pp. 715, hadiths 3567, 3568.

168 *Sahih al-Bukhari*, p. 27, hadith 68; *Sahih Muslim*, p. 1002, hadiths 2821a and c.

169 *Sahih al-Bukhari*, p. 32, hadith 90.

170 *Sunan Ibn Majah*, Vol. 1, pp. 44-45, hadith 42.

171 *Sahih al-Bukhari*, p. 33, hadith 95.

172 *Sahih al-Bukhari*, p. 1309, hadith 6645.

173 Presented here is a composite reconstruction drawn from the record in al-Waqidi, *Kitab al-Maghazi*, Vol. 3, p. 1111 and from the minutely different ahadith that capture parts of the speech: *Sahih al-Bukhari*, pp. 26-27, 35, 342, 343, 1206, 1334, 1390, 1457-1458, hadiths 67, 105, 1739, 1741, 1742, 6043, 6785, 7078, 7447; *Sunan Ibn Majah*, Vol. 3, pp. 72-73, 74, hadiths 3055, 3058.

174 The sources are the same as for the previous citation.

175 The sources are the same as for the previous citation.

176 Ibn Hisham, *Al-Sirah al-Nabawiyyah*, pp. 171, 183.

177 Ibid., p. 171.

178 Ibid., pp. 186-187.

179 *Surah al-Muddathir* 74.24, 25.

180 *Surah Ya-Sin* 36.69. See also *Surah al-Anbiyah* 21.5.

181 Al-Waqidi, *Kitab al-Maghazi*, Vol. 3, p. 957.

182 *Sahih Muslim*, pp. 851-852, hadith 2362.

183 Ibid., Vol. 3, pp. 956-957.

184 Ibid., Vol. 3, pp. 957-958.

185 Cf. *Sahih al-Bukhari*, p. 858, hadith 4333.

186 Al-Waqidi, *Kitab al-Maghazi*, Vol. 3, p. 958.

187 Ibid.

188 Abu Ja'far Muhammad ibn Jarir ibn Yazid al-'abari, *Tarikh al-Rusul wa al-Muluk* (Beirut: Dar Sader, 2008 edition), Vol. 1, p. 370.

189 Fred Donner, "The Sources of Islamic Conceptions of War" in John Kelsay and James Turner Johnson, eds., *Just War and Jihad: Historical and Theoretical Perspectives on War and Peace in Western and Islamic Traditions* (Westport, CT: Greenwood Press, 1991), p. 34.

190 Al-Waqidi, *Kitab al-Maghazi*, Vol. 2, p. 642. Here الخميس means الجيش. See *Sahih al-Bukhari*, pp. 601, 729, hadiths 2991 and 3647.

191 Joel Hayward, *Warfare in the Qur'an* English Monograph Series — Book No. 14 (Amman: Royal Islamic Strategic Studies Centre / Royal Aal al-Bayt Institute for Islamic Thought, 2012).

192 Al-Waqidi, *Kitab al-Maghazi*, Vol. 3, p. 885.

193 Joel Hayward, *Civilian Immunity in Foundational Islamic Strategic Thought,* op. cit.

194 *Surah al-Anfal* 8.60. Cf. *Sahih al-Bukhari*, p. 599, hadith 2977; *Sahih Muslim*, p. 965, hadith 2724; *Sunan al-Nasa'i*, p. 58, hadith 432.

195 *Surah al-Anfal* 8.57. "فِي الْحَرْبِ" is literally "in war".

196 *Sahih al-Bukhari*, pp. 1376-1377, hadith 6998.

197   *Sahih al-Bukhari*, p. 874, hadith 4416.

198   *Sahih Muslim*, p. 965, hadith 2724.

199   *Surah al-Nisa* 4.95.

200   *Surah Muhammad* 47.20; *Surah al-Tawba* 9.42, 81, 86, 87 and 93; *Surah al-Ahzab* 33.18ff.

201   *Sahih al-Bukhari*, p. 1392, hadith 7085.

202   *Sahih al-Bukhari*, pp. 875-877, hadith 4418; *Sahih Muslim*, pp. 980-984, hadith 2769d.

203   *Sunan al-Nasa'i*, p. 518, hadith 4115.

204   Al-Waqidi, *Kitab al-Maghazi*, Vol. 1, p. 19.

205   Ibn Hisham, *Al-Sirah al-Nabawiyyah*, Vol. 4, pp. 984.

206   Ibid., p. 985.

207   *Sahih Muslim*, p. 635, hadith 1731a, b; *Sunan Ibn Majah*, Vol. 2, pp. 532-533, hadith 2858; *Jami' al-Tirmidhi*, Vol. 2, p. 279, hadith 1408.

208   *Sahih al-Bukhari*, p. 846, hadith 4261.

209   *Sunan Abu Dawud*, p. 321, hadith 2515; *Sunan al-Nasa'i*, p. 585, hadith 4200.

210   *Surah al-Ma'idah* 5.32.

211   Cf. *Surah al-Anfal* 8.16.

212   *Sahih al-Bukhari*, hadiths 3027-330:

> 7203- حَدَّثَنَا عَبْدُ اللَّهِ بْنُ مُحَمَّدٍ حَدَّثَنَا عَبْدُ الرَّزَّاقِ أَخْبَرَنَا مَعْمَرٌ عَنْ هَمَّامٍ عَنْ أَبِي هُرَيْرَةَ رَضِيَ اللَّهُ عَنْهُ عَنِ النَّبِيِّ صَلَّى اللَّهُ عَلَيْهِ وَسَلَّمَ قَالَ: هَلَكَ كِسْرَى ثُمَّ لَا يَكُونُ كِسْرَى بَعْدَهُ وَقَيْصَرُ لَيَهْلِكَنَّ ثُمَّ لَا يَكُونُ قَيْصَرُ بَعْدَهُ وَلَتُقْسَمَنَّ كُنُوزُهَا فِي سَبِيلِ اللَّهِ
>
> 3028 – (وَسَمَّى الْحَرْبَ خُدْعَةً).

"The Prophet ﷺ said, "Khosrau [the Sasanian king] will be ruined, and there will be no Khosrau after him, and Caesar will surely be ruined and there will be no Caesar after him, and you will spend their treasures in Allah's Cause." He said that 'War is deceit.'"

3029- حَدَّثَنَا أَبُو بَكْرِ بْنُ أَصْرَمَ أَخْبَرَنَا عَبْدُ اللَّهِ أَخْبَرَنَا مَعْمَرٌ عَنْ هَمَّامِ بْنِ مُنَبِّهٍ عَنْ أَبِي هُرَيْرَةَ رَضِيَ اللَّهُ عَنْهُ قَالَ : سَمَّى النَّبِيُّ صَلَّى اللَّهُ عَلَيْهِ وَسَلَّمَ الْحَرْبَ خُدْعَةً.

"Narrated by Abu Hurairah ... that the Prophet ﷺ said: "War is deceit.""

3033- حَدَّثَنَا صَدَقَةُ بْنُ الْفَضْلِ أَخْبَرَنَا ابْنُ عُيَيْنَةَ عَنْ عَمْرٍو سَمِعَ جَابِرَ بْنَ عَبْدِ اللَّهِ رَضِيَ اللَّهُ عَنْهُمَا قَالَ: قَالَ النَّبِيُّ صَلَّى اللَّهُ عَلَيْهِ وَسَلَّمَ: الْحَرْبُ خُدْعَةٌ.

"Narrated Jabir ibn 'Abdullah ...that the Prophet said: "War is deceit.""

213 *Sahih Muslim*, p. 637:

1739 - و حَدَّثَنَا عَلِيُّ بْنُ حُجْرٍ السَّعْدِيُّ وَعَمْرُو النَّاقِدُ وَزُهَيْرُ بْنُ حَرْبٍ وَاللَّفْظُ لِعَلِيٍّ وَزُهَيْرٍ قَالَ : عَلِيٌّ أَخْبَرَنَا و قَالَ الْآخَرَانِ : حَدَّثَنَا سُفْيَانُ قَالَ : سَمِعَ عَمْرٌو جَابِرًا يَقُولُ : قَالَ رَسُولُ اللَّهِ صَلَّى اللَّهُ عَلَيْهِ وَسَلَّمَ الْحَرْبُ خُدْعَةٌ.

"Sufyan said: 'Amr heard Jabir say that the Messenger of Allah said: 'War is deceit.'"

1740 - و حَدَّثَنَا مُحَمَّدُ بْنُ عَبْدِ الرَّحْمَنِ بْنِ سَهْمٍ أَخْبَرَنَا عَبْدُ اللَّهِ بْنُ الْمُبَارَكِ أَخْبَرَنَا مَعْمَرٌ عَنْ هَمَّامِ بْنِ مُنَبِّهٍ عَنْ أَبِي هُرَيْرَةَ قَالَ قَالَ رَسُولُ اللَّهِ صَلَّى اللَّهُ عَلَيْهِ وَسَلَّمَ الْحَرْبُ خُدْعَةٌ.

"It was narrated from Abu Hurairah that the Messenger of Allah said: 'War is deceit.'"

214 *Sunan Ibn Majah*, Vol. 2, p. 523, hadiths 2833 and 2834:

2833- حَدَّثَنَا مُحَمَّدُ بْنُ عَبْدِ اللَّهِ بْنِ نُمَيْرٍ، حَدَّثَنَا يُونُسُ بْنُ بُكَيْرٍ، عَنْ مُحَمَّدِ بْنِ إِسْحَاقَ، عَنْ يَزِيدَ بْنِ رُومَانَ، عَنْ عُرْوَةَ، عَنْ عَائِشَةَ، أَنَّ النَّبِيَّ صلى الله عليه وسلم قَالَ " الْحَرْبُ خُدْعَةٌ".

"It was narrated on the authority of ... A'ishah that the Prophet ﷺ said: "War is deceit.""

2834- حَدَّثَنَا مُحَمَّدُ بْنُ عَبْدِ اللَّهِ بْنِ نُمَيْرٍ، حَدَّثَنَا يُونُسُ بْنُ بُكَيْرٍ، عَنْ مَطَرِ بْنِ مَيْمُونٍ، عَنْ عِكْرِمَةَ، عَنِ ابْنِ عَبَّاسٍ، أَنَّ النَّبِيَّ صلى الله عليه وسلم قَالَ " الْحَرْبُ خُدْعَةٌ".

"It was narrated on the authority of ... Ibn 'Abbas that the Prophet ﷺ said: "War is deceit.""

215   *Sunan Abu Dawud*, pp. 387-389, hadiths 2369 and 2370:

2369- حَدَّثَنَا سَعِيدُ بْنُ مَنْصُورٍ، حَدَّثَنَا سُفْيَانُ، عَنْ عَمْرٍو، أَنَّهُ سَمِعَ جَابِرًا، أَنَّ رَسُولَ اللَّهِ صلى الله عليه وسلم قَالَ " الْحَرْبُ خُدْعَةٌ ".

"Jabir reported … the Prophet ﷺ as saying that "War is deception."

2370- حَدَّثَنَا مُحَمَّدُ بْنُ عُبَيْدٍ، حَدَّثَنَا ابْنُ ثَوْرٍ، عَنْ مَعْمَرٍ، عَنِ الزُّهْرِيِّ، عَنْ عَبْدِ الرَّحْمَنِ بْنِ كَعْبِ بْنِ مَالِكٍ، عَنْ أَبِيهِ، أَنَّ النَّبِيَّ صلى الله عليه وسلم كَانَ إِذَا أَرَادَ غَزْوَةً وَرَّى غَيْرَهَا وَكَانَ يَقُولُ " الْحَرْبُ خُدْعَةٌ " . قَالَ أَبُو دَاوُدَ لَمْ يَجِئْ بِهِ إِلاَّ مَعْمَرٌ يُرِيدُ قَوْلَهُ " الْحَرْبُ خُدْعَةٌ ". بِهَذَا الإِسْنَادِ إِنَّمَا يُرْوَى مِنْ حَدِيثِ عَمْرِو بْنِ دِينَارٍ عَنْ جَابِرٍ وَمِنْ حَدِيثِ مَعْمَرٍ عَنْ هَمَّامِ بْنِ مُنَبِّهٍ عَنْ أَبِي هُرَيْرَةَ .

"Narrated Ka'b ibn Malik: When the Prophet ﷺ intended to go on an expedition, he always pretended to be going somewhere else, and he would say: War is deception. Abu Dawud said: Only Ma'mar has transmitted this tradition. By this he refers to his statement 'War is deception' through this chain of narrators. He narrated it from the tradition of 'Amr ibn Dinar from Jabir, and from the tradition of Ma'mar from Hammam ibn Munabbih on the authority of Abu Hurairah."

216   *Jami' al-Tirmidhi*, p. 408, hadith 1675:

1675- حَدَّثَنَا أَحْمَدُ بْنُ مَنِيعٍ، وَنَصْرُ بْنُ عَلِيٍّ، قَالاَ حَدَّثَنَا سُفْيَانُ بْنُ عُيَيْنَةَ، عَنْ عَمْرِو بْنِ دِينَارٍ، سَمِعَ جَابِرَ بْنَ عَبْدِ اللَّهِ، يَقُولُ قَالَ رَسُولُ اللَّهِ صلى الله عليه وسلم " الْحَرْبُ خُدْعَةٌ " . قَالَ أَبُو عِيسَى وَفِي الْبَابِ عَنْ عَلِيٍّ وَزَيْدِ بْنِ ثَابِتٍ وَعَائِشَةَ وَابْنِ عَبَّاسٍ وَأَبِي هُرَيْرَةَ وَأَسْمَاءَ بِنْتِ يَزِيدَ بْنِ السَّكَنِ وَكَعْبِ بْنِ مَالِكٍ وَأَنَسِ بْنِ مَالِكٍ . وَهَذَا حَدِيثٌ حَسَنٌ صَحِيحٌ .

"Narrated Jabir ibn 'Abdullah that That the Messenger of Allah (ﷺ) said: 'War is deceit.' [Abu 'Eisa said:] There are narrations on this topic from 'Ali, Zaid ibn Thabit, 'Aishah, Ibn 'Abbas, Abu Hurairah, Asma bint Yazid ibn As-Sakan, Ka'b ibn Malik and Anas ibn Malik. This hadith is Hasan Sahih."

217   Al-Waqidi, *Kitab al-Maghazi*, Vol. 3, p. 990.

218   Ibid., Vol. 1, p. 13; Ibn Hisham, *Al-Sirah al-Nabawiyyah*, Vol. 2, p. 214.

219   Cf. Al-Waqidi, *Kitab al-Maghazi*, Vol. 2, pp. 534, 564, 728, 753,

Endnotes

755, 778, Vol. 3, p. 981.

220   Ibid., Vol. 1, p. 342.
221   Fred Donner, "Sources of Islamic Conceptions of War," pp. 34-35.
222   Ibid., Vol. 1, p. 299.
223   Ibn Hisham, *Al-Sirah al-Nabawiyyah*, Vol. 3, pp. 389-390.
224   Al-Waqidi, *Kitab al-Maghazi*, Vol. 1, p. 338.
225   Ibn Hisham, *Al-Sirah al-Nabawiyyah*, Vol. 3, pp. 589-590.
226   Al-Waqidi, *Kitab al-Maghazi*, Vol. 2, pp. 486-487.
227   Ibid., Vol. 2, pp. 488-489.
228   Ibid., Vol. 2, p. 536.
229   Ibid., Vol. 2, p. 585.
230   Ibn Hisham, *Al-Sirah al-Nabawiyyah*, Vol. 3, pp. 359.
231   Al-Waqidi, *Kitab al-Maghazi*, Vol. 2, p. 642.
232   Ibid., Vol. 2, p. 796.
233   Ibid.
234   Ibid.
235   Ibid.
236   Ibid., Vol. 2, p. 814.
237   Ibid., Vol. 2, p. 758.
238   *Surah al-Hajj* 22.40.
239   Ibn Hisham, *Al-Sirah al-Nabawiyyah*, p. 972.
240   Al-Waqidi, *Kitab al-Maghazi*, Vol. 1, pp. 145-146, 300-307, Vol. 2, p. 769, Vol. 3, p. 922; Ibn Hisham, *Al-Sirah al-Nabawiyyah*, Vol. 2, pp. 364-365, Vol. 3, pp. 129-133, Vol. 4, pp. 30, 101.
241   Al-Waqidi, *Kitab al-Maghazi*, Vol. 2, pp. 699-600.
242   Al-Waqidi, *Kitab al-Maghazi*, Vol. 2, pp. 495-496.
243   *Sahih al-Bukhari*, p. 31-32, hadith 89.

244   *Sahih al-Bukhari*, p. 132, hadith 631:

حَدَّثَنَا مُحَمَّدُ بْنُ الْمُثَنَّى، قَالَ حَدَّثَنَا عَبْدُ الْوَهَّابِ، قَالَ حَدَّثَنَا أَيُّوبُ، عَنْ أَبِي قِلاَبَةَ، قَالَ حَدَّثَنَا مَالِكٌ، أَتَيْنَا إِلَى النَّبِيِّ صلى الله عليه وسلم وَنَحْنُ شَبَبَةٌ مُتَقَارِبُونَ، فَأَقَمْنَا عِنْدَهُ عِشْرِينَ يَوْمًا وَلَيْلَةً، وَكَانَ رَسُولُ اللَّهِ صلى الله عليه وسلم رَحِيمًا رَفِيقًا، فَلَمَّا ظَنَّ أَنَّا قَدِ اشْتَهَيْنَا أَهْلَنَا أَوْ قَدِ اشْتَقْنَا سَأَلَنَا عَمَّنْ تَرَكْنَا بَعْدَنَا فَأَخْبَرْنَاهُ قَالَ " ارْجِعُوا إِلَى أَهْلِيكُمْ فَأَقِيمُوا فِيهِمْ وَعَلِّمُوهُمْ وَمُرُوهُمْ ـ وَذَكَرَ أَشْيَاءَ أَحْفَظُهَا أَوْ لاَ أَحْفَظُهَا ـ وَصَلُّوا كَمَا رَأَيْتُمُونِي أُصَلِّي، فَإِذَا حَضَرَتِ الصَّلاَةُ فَلْيُؤَذِّنْ لَكُمْ أَحَدُكُمْ وَلْيَؤُمَّكُمْ أَكْبَرُكُمْ ".

245   *Sahih al-Bukhari,* p. 602, hadith 2997.

246   *Sahih al-Bukhari,* p. 813, hadith 4077.

247   Ibn Hisham, *Al-Sirah al-Nabawiyyah*, Vol. 3, pp. 589.

248   *Sahih al-Bukhari,* p. 1280, hadith 6465.

249   *Sahih al-Bukhari,* p. 1306, hadith 6622:

حَدَّثَنَا أَبُو النُّعْمَانِ، مُحَمَّدُ بْنُ الْفَضْلِ حَدَّثَنَا جَرِيرُ بْنُ حَازِمٍ، حَدَّثَنَا الْحَسَنُ، عَبْدَ الرَّحْمَنِ بْنَ سَمُرَةَ، قَالَ قَالَ النَّبِيُّ صلى الله عليه وسلم " يَا عَبْدَ الرَّحْمَنِ بْنَ سَمُرَةَ لاَ تَسْأَلِ الإِمَارَةَ، فَإِنَّكَ إِنْ أُوتِيتَهَا عَنْ مَسْأَلَةٍ وُكِلْتَ إِلَيْهَا، وَإِنْ أُوتِيتَهَا مِنْ غَيْرِ مَسْأَلَةٍ أُعِنْتَ عَلَيْهَا، وَإِذَا حَلَفْتَ عَلَى يَمِينٍ فَرَأَيْتَ غَيْرَهَا خَيْرًا مِنْهَا، فَكَفِّرْ عَنْ يَمِينِكَ، وَأْتِ الَّذِي هُوَ خَيْرٌ ".

250   Cf. *Sahih al-Bukhari*, pp. 595, hadith 2957.

251   *Sunan Abu Dawud*, p. 330, hadith 2608:

حَدَّثَنَا عَلِيُّ بْنُ بَحْرِ بْنِ بَرِّيٍّ، حَدَّثَنَا حَاتِمُ بْنُ إِسْمَاعِيلَ، حَدَّثَنَا مُحَمَّدُ بْنُ عَجْلاَنَ، عَنْ نَافِعٍ، عَنْ أَبِي سَلَمَةَ، عَنْ أَبِي سَعِيدٍ الْخُدْرِيِّ، أَنَّ رَسُولَ اللَّهِ صلى الله عليه وسلم قَالَ " إِذَا خَرَجَ ثَلاَثَةٌ فِي سَفَرٍ فَلْيُؤَمِّرُوا أَحَدَهُمْ."

252   Ibn Hisham, *Al-Sirah al-Nabawiyyah*, pp. 217-219.

253   Ibid., pp. 289-290.

254   Ibid., p. 843.

255   *Sahih al-Bukhari*, p. 1193, hadith 5964.

255   Al-Waqidi, *Kitab al-Maghazi*, Vol. 2, p. 834; *Sahih al-Bukhari*, pp. 110, 850, hadiths 504; 4289.

257 Ibn Hisham, *Al-Sirah al-Nabawiyyah*, p. 984; Al-Waqidi, *Kitab al-Maghazi*, Vol. 2, pp. 724-725.

258 Al-Waqidi, *Kitab al-Maghazi*, Vol. 3, pp. 1117-1119; Ibn Sa'd, *Kitab al-Tabaqat al-Kabir*, Vol. 2, p. 312; *Sahih al-Bukhari*, pp. 747, 884, 1409, hadiths 3730, 4469, 7187; *Sahih Muslim*, p. 874, hadith 2426a.

259 *Sahih al-Bukhari*, p. 1285, hadith 6496:

حَدَّثَنَا مُحَمَّدُ بْنُ سِنَانٍ، حَدَّثَنَا فُلَيْحُ بْنُ سُلَيْمَانَ، حَدَّثَنَا هِلَالُ بْنُ عَلِيٍّ، عَنْ عَطَاءِ بْنِ يَسَارٍ، عَنْ أَبِي هُرَيْرَةَ ـ رضى الله عنه ـ قَالَ قَالَ رَسُولُ اللَّهِ صلى الله عليه وسلم " إِذَا ضُيِّعَتِ الأَمَانَةُ فَانْتَظِرِ السَّاعَةَ ". قَالَ كَيْفَ إِضَاعَتُهَا يَا رَسُولَ اللَّهِ قَالَ " إِذَا أُسْنِدَ الأَمْرُ إِلَى غَيْرِ أَهْلِهِ، فَانْتَظِرِ السَّاعَةَ".

Cf. *Sahih al-Bukhari*, p. 24, hadith 59; *Riyad al-Salihin*, hadith 1837.

260 *Sahih Muslim*, p. 675, hadith 1825; *Sunan al-Nasa'i*, p. 518, hadith 3697.

261 *Sahih al-Bukhari*, pp. 756-757, 138, hadiths 3792, 7057; *Jami' al-Tirmidhi*, Vol. 3, p. 177, hadith 2189.

262 Al-Waqidi, *Kitab al-Maghazi*, Vol. 2, pp. 754-755.

263 Ella Landau-Tasseron, "Features of the Pre-conquest Muslim Army in the Time of Muhammad," in Averil Cameron, ed., *Studies in Late Antiquity and Early Islam: The Byzantine and Early Islamic Near East*, III (Princeton NJ: The Darwin Press, 1995), pp. 299-336, esp. p. 317.

264 Al-Waqidi, *Kitab al-Maghazi*, Vol. 2, pp. 741, 750.

265 Ibn Hisham, *Al-Sirah al-Nabawiyyah*, pp. 984-985; Al-Waqidi, *Kitab al-Maghazi*, Vol. 2, p. 770.

266 Ibid., Vol. 2, p. 770.

267 Ibn Hisham, *Al-Sirah al-Nabawiyyah*, p. 823.

268 Ibid., pp. 833-836; Al-Waqidi, *Kitab al-Maghazi*, Vol. 3, pp. 875-876.

269 Ibn Hisham, *Al-Sirah al-Nabawiyyah*, p. 835. Cf. *Sahih al-*

Bukhari, pp. 859, 1409-1410, hadiths 7189, 4339; *Sunan al-Nasa'i*, p. 734, hadith 5407.

270 Al-Waqidi, *Kitab al-Maghazi*, Vol. 3, p. 882.

271 Ibn Hisham, *Al-Sirah al-Nabawiyyah*, p. 835. Cf. *Sahih Muslim*, p. 909, hadith 2541a.

272 *Sunan Abu Dawud*, p. 337, 2669:

حَدَّثَنَا أَبُو الْوَلِيدِ الطَّيَالِسِيُّ، حَدَّثَنَا عُمَرُ بْنُ الْمُرَقَّعِ بْنِ صَيْفِيِّ بْنِ رَبَاحٍ، حَدَّثَنِي أَبِي، عَنْ جَدِّهِ، رَبَاحِ بْنِ رَبِيعٍ قَالَ كُنَّا مَعَ رَسُولِ اللَّهِ صلى الله عليه وسلم فِي غَزْوَةٍ فَرَأَى النَّاسَ مُجْتَمِعِينَ عَلَى شَىْءٍ فَبَعَثَ رَجُلاً فَقَالَ " انْظُرْ عَلاَمَ اجْتَمَعَ هَؤُلاَءِ " فَجَاءَ فَقَالَ عَلَى امْرَأَةٍ قَتِيلٍ . فَقَالَ " مَا كَانَتْ هَذِهِ لِتُقَاتِلَ " . قَالَ وَعَلَى الْمُقَدِّمَةِ خَالِدُ بْنُ الْوَلِيدِ فَبَعَثَ رَجُلاً فَقَالَ " قُلْ لِخَالِدٍ لاَ يَقْتُلَنَّ امْرَأَةً وَلاَ عَسِيفًا " .

Cf. *Sunan Ibn Majah*, Vol. 2, p. 526, hadith 2842; *Sahih al-Bukhari*, p. 605, hadiths 3014, 3015; *Sahih Muslim*, p. 637, 638, hadiths 1744a; 1744b.

273 Al-Waqidi, *Kitab al-Maghazi*, Vol. 2, p. 722.

274 Al-Waqidi, *Kitab al-Maghazi*, Vol. 1, pp. 342, 343.

275 Al-Waqidi, *Kitab al-Maghazi*, Vol. 2, p. 728.

276 *Sunan Abu Dawud*, p. 453, hadith 3592.

277 *Sahih al-Bukhari*, p. 860, hadiths 4341, 4342; Ibn Hisham, *Al-Sirah al-Nabawiyyah*, p. 957.

278 Al-Waqidi, *Kitab al-Maghazi*, Vol. 1, p. 215.

279 *Sahih al-Bukhari*, p. 791, hadiths 3955; 3956.

280 *Sahih al-Bukhari*, pp. 599, 743, 839, hadiths 2975, 3702, 4209.

281 *Sahih al-Bukhari*, p. 615, hadith 3063.

282 *Sahih al-Bukhari*, p. 846, hadith 4262. Interestingly, this single hadith names Khalid as "the sword among Allah's swords" (سَيْفٌ مِنْ سُيُوفِ اللَّهِ). *The same* phrase is found in Al-Waqidi, *Kitab al-Maghazi*, Vol. 3, p. 883.

283 Ibn Hisham, *Al-Sirah al-Nabawiyyah*, pp. 880-881.

284   Ibid., p. 982.

285   *Sunan Abu Dawud*, p. 332, hadith 2627:

حَدَّثَنَا يَحْيَى بْنُ مَعِينٍ، حَدَّثَنَا عَبْدُ الصَّمَدِ بْنُ عَبْدِ الْوَارِثِ، حَدَّثَنَا سُلَيْمَانُ بْنُ الْمُغِيرَةِ، حَدَّثَنَا حُمَيْدُ بْنُ هِلاَلٍ، عَنْ بِشْرِ بْنِ عَاصِمٍ، عَنْ عُقْبَةَ بْنِ مَالِكٍ، مِنْ رَهْطِهِ قَالَ بَعَثَ النَّبِيُّ صلى الله عليه وسلم سَرِيَّةً فَسَلَحْتُ رَجُلاً مِنْهُمْ سَيْفًا فَلَمَّا رَجَعَ قَالَ لَوْ رَأَيْتَ مَا لاَمَنَا رَسُولُ اللَّهِ صلى الله عليه وسلم قَالَ " أَعَجَزْتُمْ إِذْ بَعَثْتُ رَجُلاً مِنْكُمْ فَلَمْ يَمْضِ لأَمْرِي أَنْ تَجْعَلُوا مَكَانَهُ مَنْ يَمْضِي لأَمْرِي ".

286   *Sahih al-Bukhari*, p. 596, hadith 2964.

287   Al-Waqidi, *Kitab al-Maghazi*, Vol. 3, p. 873.

288   *Sahih al-Bukhari*, p. 1428, hadith 7288.

289   *Jami' al-Tirmidhi*, Vol. 2, pp. 286-287, hadith 1424. Opinions differ regarding the reliability of this hadith's isnad.

290   *Sahih al-Bukhari*, p. 482, hadith 2442.

291   *Jami' al-Tirmidhi*, Vol. 3, p. 90, hadith 2015.

292   Ibn Hisham, *Al-Sirah al-Nabawiyyah*, p. 798.

293   Al-Waqidi, *Kitab al-Maghazi*, Vol. 2, p. 613.

294   Ibn Hisham, *Al-Sirah al-Nabawiyyah*, pp. 809-810; Al-Waqidi, *Kitab al-Maghazi*, Vol. 2, pp. 797-798.

295   Ibn Hisham, *Al-Sirah al-Nabawiyyah*, p. 816. See the subtle retelling of this story in *Sahih al-Bukhari*, p. 849, hadith 4280.

296   Al-Waqidi, *Kitab al-Maghazi*, Vol. 2, pp. 681-682.

297   *Sahih Muslim*, p. 679, hadith 1833a; *Sunan Abu Dawud*, p. 452, hadith 3581.

298   *Sunan Abu Dawud*, pp. 376-377, hadith 2946:

حَدَّثَنَا ابْنُ السَّرْحِ، وَابْنُ أَبِي خَلَفٍ، - لَفْظُهُ - قَالاَ حَدَّثَنَا سُفْيَانُ، عَنِ الزُّهْرِيِّ، عَنْ عُرْوَةَ، عَنْ أَبِي حُمَيْدٍ السَّاعِدِيِّ، أَنَّ النَّبِيَّ صلى الله عليه وسلم اسْتَعْمَلَ رَجُلاً مِنَ الأَزْدِ يُقَالُ لَهُ ابْنُ اللُّتْبِيَّةِ - قَالَ ابْنُ السَّرْحِ ابْنُ الأُتْبِيَّةِ - عَلَى الصَّدَقَةِ فَجَاءَ فَقَالَ هَذَا لَكُمْ وَهَذَا أُهْدِيَ لِي . فَقَامَ النَّبِيُّ صلى الله عليه وسلم عَلَى الْمِنْبَرِ فَحَمِدَ اللَّهَ وَأَثْنَى عَلَيْهِ وَقَالَ " مَا بَالُ الْعَامِلِ نَبْعَثُهُ فَيَجِيءُ فَيَقُولُ هَذَا لَكُمْ وَهَذَا أُهْدِيَ لِي

. أَلَا جَلَسَ فِي بَيْتِ أُمِّهِ أَوْ أَبِيهِ فَيَنْظُرَ أَيُهْدَى لَهُ أَمْ لَا لَا يَأْتِي أَحَدٌ مِنْكُمْ بِشَيْءٍ مِنْ ذَلِكَ إِلَّا جَاءَ بِهِ يَوْمَ الْقِيَامَةِ إِنْ كَانَ بَعِيرًا فَلَهُ رُغَاءٌ أَوْ بَقَرَةً فَلَهَا خُوَارٌ أَوْ شَاةً تَيْعَرُ ". ثُمَّ رَفَعَ يَدَيْهِ حَتَّى رَأَيْنَا عُفْرَةَ إِبْطَيْهِ ثُمَّ قَالَ " اللَّهُمَّ هَلْ بَلَّغْتُ اللَّهُمَّ هَلْ بَلَّغْتُ".

Cf. *Sahih al-Bukhari*, pp. 1407, 1412, hadiths 7174, 7197; *Sahih Muslim*, p. 678, hadith 1832.

299   Al-Waqidi, *Kitab al-Maghazi*, Vol. 1, pp. 304-305.

300   Hans J. Morgenthau, *Politics among Nations: The Struggle for Power and Peace* (New York: Alfred A. Knopf, 1948).

301   Halil İbrahim Hançabay, "The Meeting of the Prophet Muhammad with a Delegation of Christians from Najrān and the Incident of Mubāhala", *The Islamic Quarterly*, Vol. 59, No. 3 (2015), pp. 291-314.

302   Ibn Sa'd, *Kitab al-Tabaqat al-Kabir*, Vol. 1, p. 419.

303   Ibn Sa'd, *Kitab al-Tabaqat al-Kabir*, Vol. 1, p. 419; *Sunan Abu Dawud*, p. 389, hadith 3041.

304   Ibn Hisham, *Al-Sirah al-Nabawiyyah*, pp. 410-411; *Sahih al-Bukhari*, p. 1422, hadith 7254.

305   *Sunan Abu Dawud*, pp. 349, 350, hadiths 2758, 2761.

306   M. Cherif Bassiouni, "Protection of Diplomats under Islamic Law", *The American Journal of International Law*, Vol. 74, No. 3 (July 1980), pp. 609-633.

307   *Sahih al-Bukhari*, p. 1357, hadith 6914:

حَدَّثَنَا قَيْسُ بْنُ حَفْصٍ، حَدَّثَنَا عَبْدُ الْوَاحِدِ، حَدَّثَنَا الْحَسَنُ، حَدَّثَنَا مُجَاهِدٌ، عَنْ عَبْدِ اللَّهِ بْنِ عَمْرٍو، عَنِ النَّبِيِّ صلى الله عليه وسلم قَالَ "مَنْ قَتَلَ نَفْسًا مُعَاهَدًا لَمْ يَرَحْ رَائِحَةَ الْجَنَّةِ، وَإِنَّ رِيحَهَا يُوجَدُ مِنْ مَسِيرَةِ أَرْبَعِينَ عَامًا".

308   Al-Waqidi, *Kitab al-Maghazi*, Vol. 2, pp. 603-604.

309   Surah al-Nahl 16.125.

310   Surah Ta-Ha 20.44.

311   Ibn Hisham, *Al-Sirah al-Nabawiyyah*, p. 880.

312 Al-Waqidi, *Kitab al-Maghazi*, Vol. 2, pp. 854, 855.

313 *Sahih al-Bukhari*, p. 862, hadith 4351; *Sahih Muslim*, pp. 353-354, hadith 1064b.

314 Ibn Sa'd, *Kitab al-Tabaqat al-Kabir*, Vol. 1, pp. 349, 353, 354 and other pp.

315 *Surah Ibrahim* 14.37.

316 *Surah al-Baqarah* 2.256.

317 *Surah al-Ma'idah* 5.1. See also *Surah al-Baqarah* 2.177.

318 Al-Waqidi, *Kitab al-Maghazi*, Vol. 2, 780-795.

319 *Surah al-Tawba* 9.6.

320 Fred Donner, "Mecca's Food Supplies and Muhammad's Boycott," *Journal of the Economic and* Social History of the Orient, Vol. 20, No. 3 (October 1977), pp. 249-266.

321 Ibn Hisham, *Al-Sirah al-Nabawiyyah*, pp. 958-959.

322 Cf. *Jami' al-Tirmidhi*, Vol. 3, p. 526, hadith 1548 (emphasis added):

Abu al-Bakhtari narrated that an army of the Muslims, commanded by Salman al-Farasi, besieged one of the Persian fortresses. They said: 'O Abu 'Abdullah! Should we attack them?' He said: 'Leave me to call them [to Islam] as I heard the Messenger of Allah ﷺ call them.' So Salman went to them and said: 'I am only a man from among you, a Persian, and you see that the Arabs obey me. If you become Muslims then you will have the likes of what we have, and from you will be required that which is required from us. If you refuse, and keep your religion, then we will leave you to it, and you will give us jizya from your hands while you are submissive.' He said to them in Persian: 'And you are other than praiseworthy and if you refuse then we will equally resist you.' They said: 'We will not give you jizya. We will fight you instead.' So they said: 'O Abu 'Abdullah! Should we attack them?' He said: 'No.'" He said: "So for three days he made the same call to Islam, and then he said: 'Attack them.'" He said: "So we attacked them, and we conquered the fortress."

حَدَّثَنَا قُتَيْبَةُ، حَدَّثَنَا أَبُو عَوَانَةَ، عَنْ عَطَاءِ بْنِ السَّائِبِ، عَنْ أَبِي الْبَخْتَرِيِّ، أَنَّ جَيْشًا مِنْ جُيُوشِ الْمُسْلِمِينَ كَانَ أَمِيرَهُمْ سَلْمَانُ الْفَارِسِيُّ حَاصَرُوا قَصْرًا مِنْ قُصُورِ فَارِسَ فَقَالُوا يَا أَبَا عَبْدِ اللَّهِ أَلاَ نَنْهَدُ إِلَيْهِمْ قَالَ دَعُونِي أَدْعُهُمْ كَمَا سَمِعْتُ رَسُولَ اللَّهِ صلى الله عليه وسلم يَدْعُوهُمْ . فَأَتَاهُمْ سَلْمَانُ فَقَالَ لَهُمْ إِنَّمَا أَنَا رَجُلٌ مِنْكُمْ فَارِسِيٌّ تَرَوْنَ الْعَرَبَ يُطِيعُونَنِي فَإِنْ أَسْلَمْتُمْ فَلَكُمْ مِثْلُ الَّذِي لَنَا وَعَلَيْكُمْ مِثْلُ الَّذِي عَلَيْنَا وَإِنْ أَبَيْتُمْ إِلاَّ دِينَكُمْ تَرَكْنَاكُمْ عَلَيْهِ وَأَعْطُونَا الْجِزْيَةَ عَنْ يَدٍ وَأَنْتُمْ صَاغِرُونَ. قَالَ وَرَطَنَ إِلَيْهِمْ بِالْفَارِسِيَّةِ وَأَنْتُمْ غَيْرُ مَحْمُودِينَ . وَإِنْ أَبَيْتُمْ نَابَذْنَاكُمْ عَلَى سَوَاءٍ . قَالُوا مَا نَحْنُ بِالَّذِي نُعْطِي الْجِزْيَةَ وَلَكِنَّا نُقَاتِلُكُمْ . فَقَالُوا يَا أَبَا عَبْدِ اللَّهِ أَلاَ نَنْهَدُ إِلَيْهِمْ قَالَ لاَ . فَدَعَاهُمْ ثَلاَثَةَ أَيَّامٍ إِلَى مِثْلِ هَذَا ثُمَّ قَالَ انْهَدُوا إِلَيْهِمْ . قَالَ فَنَهَدْنَا إِلَيْهِمْ فَفَتَحْنَا ذَلِكَ الْقَصْرَ . قَالَ وَفِي الْبَابِ عَنْ بُرَيْدَةَ وَالنُّعْمَانِ بْنِ مُقَرِّنٍ وَابْنِ عُمَرَ وَابْنِ عَبَّاسٍ . وَحَدِيثُ سَلْمَانَ حَدِيثٌ حَسَنٌ لاَ نَعْرِفُهُ إِلاَّ مِنْ حَدِيثِ عَطَاءِ بْنِ السَّائِبِ . وَسَمِعْتُ مُحَمَّدًا يَقُولُ أَبُو الْبَخْتَرِيِّ لَمْ يُدْرِكْ سَلْمَانَ لأَنَّهُ لَمْ يُدْرِكْ عَلِيًّا وَسَلْمَانُ مَاتَ قَبْلَ عَلِيٍّ . وَقَدْ ذَهَبَ بَعْضُ أَهْلِ الْعِلْمِ مِنْ أَصْحَابِ النَّبِيِّ صلى الله عليه وسلم إِلَى هَذَا وَرَأَوْا أَنْ يُدْعَوْا قَبْلَ الْقِتَالِ وَهُوَ قَوْلُ إِسْحَاقَ بْنِ إِبْرَاهِيمَ قَالَ إِنْ تُقَدِّمَ إِلَيْهِمْ فِي الدَّعْوَةِ فَحَسَنٌ يَكُونُ ذَلِكَ أَهْيَبَ . وَقَالَ بَعْضُ أَهْلِ الْعِلْمِ لاَ دَعْوَةَ الْيَوْمَ . وَقَالَ أَحْمَدُ لاَ أَعْرِفُ الْيَوْمَ أَحَدًا يُدْعَى. وَقَالَ الشَّافِعِيُّ لاَ يُقَاتَلُ الْعَدُوُّ حَتَّى يُدْعَوْا إِلاَّ أَنْ يَعْجَلُوا عَنْ ذَلِكَ فَإِنْ لَمْ يَفْعَلْ فَقَدْ بَلَغَتْهُمُ الدَّعْوَةُ.

323   *Sahih Muslim*, p. 635, hadith 1731a, b.

324   Ibid., p. 960.

325   Martin van Creveld, *Command in War* (Cambridge, Mass: Harvard University Press, 1985), p. 64.

326   *Jami' al-Tirmidhi*, Vol. 3, p. 333, hadith 2517.

Bibliography

Hadith Collections

Sahih al-Bukhari (Cairo: Dar Al-Afaq al-Arabia, 2004).

Sahih Muslim (Cairo: Dar Al-Ghad Al-Gadid, 2007).

Sunan Abu Dawud (Riyadh: Dar al-Haddarah lil-Nasha wa al-Tawziyyah, 2015).

Sunan Ibn Majah (Cairo: Dar al-Hadith, 2005).

Sunan al-Nasa'i (Riyadh: Darussalam, 1999).

Jami' al-Tirmidhi (Beirut: Dar al-Kutub al-Ilmiyah, 2008).

Al-Adab Al-Mufrad (Beirut: Dar Al-Kotob Al-Ilmiyah, 2004).

Other Works

Adair, John, *The Leadership of Muhammad* (London: Kogan Page, 2010).

Ahmed, Ziauddin, "Financial Policies of the Holy Prophet: A Case Study of the Distribution of Ghanima in Early Islam", *Islamic Studies*, Vol. 14, No. 1 (Spring 1975).

Al-Azami, Nabeel, *Muhammad ﷺ: 11 Leadership Qualities That Changed the World* (Swansea: Claritas Books, 2019).

Al-Waqadi, *Kitab al-Maghazi* (Beirut: Muassassat al-'Alami, 1989).

Bassiouni, M. Cherif, "Protection of Diplomats under Islamic Law", *The American Journal of International Law*, Vol. 74, No. 3 (July 1980), pp. 609-633.

Beekun, Rafik Issa and Jamal A. Badawi, *Leadership: An Islamic Perspective* (Maryland: Amana, 1999).

Brown, Jonathan A. C., *Hadith: Muhammad's Legacy in the Medieval and Modern World* (Oxford: Oneworld, 2009. 2011 edition).

Donner, Fred, "Mecca's Food Supplies and Muhammad's Boycott," *Journal of the Economic and Social History of the Orient*, Vol. 20, No. 3 (October 1977), pp. 249-266.

--, *Muhammad and the Believers at the Origins of Islam* (Cambridge, Mass, and London: Belknap Press of Harvard University Press, 2010).

--, *The Early Islamic Conquests* (Princeton University Press, 1981).

--, "The Sources of Islamic Conceptions of War" in John Kelsay and James Turner Johnson, eds., *Just War and Jihad: Historical and Theoretical Perspectives on War and Peace in Western and Islamic Traditions* (Westport, CT: Greenwood Press, 1991), pp. 31-69.

El-Sharif, Ahmad, "What can the Prophet Muhammad's Metaphors Do?" *Advances in Language and Literary Studies*, Vol. 5, No. 5 (October 2018), pp. 69-78.

Hançabay, Halil İbrahim, "The Meeting of the Prophet Muhammad with a Delegation of Christians from Najrān and the Incident of Mubāhala", *The Islamic Quarterly*, Vol. 59, No. 3 (2015), pp. 291-314.

Hayward, Joel, *Civilian Immunity in Foundational Islamic Strategic Thought: A Historical Enquiry* (Amman: The Royal Islamic Strategic Studies Centre, 2016).

--, *Warfare in the Qur'an* English Monograph Series — Book No. 14 (Amman: Royal Islamic Strategic Studies Centre / Royal Aal al-Bayt Institute for Islamic Thought, 2012).

Hoyland, Robert G., *Seeing Islam as Others Saw It: A Survey of Christian, Jewish and Zoroastrian Writings on Early Islam* (Piscataway, NJ: Gorgias Press, 2019 edition).

Ibn Hisham, *Al-Sirah al-Nabawiyyah* (Beirut: Maktaba Allassrya, 2012).

Ibn Sa'd, *Kitab al-Tabaqat al-Kabir* (Kitab Bhavan, 2009 ed.).

Bibliography

Jones, Linda G., *The Power of Oratory in the Medieval Muslim World* (Cambridge University Press, 2012).

Landau-Tasseron, Ella, "Features of the Pre-conquest Muslim Army in the Time of Muhammad," in Averil Cameron, ed., *Studies in Late Antiquity and Early Islam: The Byzantine and Early Islamic Near East*, III (Princeton NJ: The Darwin Press, 1995), pp. 299-336, esp. p. 317.

--, *The Religious Foundations of Political Allegiance: A Study of Bay'a in Pre-modern Islam* Research Monographs on the Muslim World, Series No 2, Paper No 4, May, 2010 (Washington DC: Hudson Institute).

Lane, Edward William, *An Arabic-English Lexicon Derived from the Best and Most Copious Eastern Sources* (London: Willams & Norgate 1863).

Lecker, Michael, *The Constitution of Medina: Muhammad's First Legal Document* (Princeton, NJ: Darwin, 2004).

--, "The Hudaybiyya-Treaty and the Expedition against Khaybar," *Jerusalem Studies in Arabic and Islam*, Vol. 5 (1984), pp. 1-11.

Mernissi, Fatema, *Women and Islam: An Historical and Theological Enquiry* Translated by Mary Jo Lakeland (Oxford: Blackwell, 1987).

Morgenthau, Hans J., *Politics among Nations: The Struggle for Power and Peace* (New York: Alfred A. Knopf, 1948).

Nazeer Ka Ka Khel, Muhammad, "The Conceptual and Institutional Development of Shura in Early Islam", *Islamic Studies*, Vol. 19, No. 4 (Winter 1980), pp. 271-282.

Pourshariati, Parvaneh, *Decline and Fall of the Sasanian Empire: The Sasanian-Parthian Confederacy and the Arab Conquest of Iran* (London: I. B. Taurus, 2008).

Van Creveld, Martin, *Command in War* (Cambridge, Mass: Harvard University Press, 1985).

Wadud, Amina, *Quran and Woman: Re-Reading the Sacred Text from a Woman's Perspective* (New York: Oxford University Press, 1999).

Index

'Abdullah ibn Anys 111
'Abdullah ibn Hudhafa ibn Qais ibn 'Adi 31
'Abdullah ibn Jahsh 89
'Abdullah ibn Khaythama al-Salami 48
'Abdullah ibn Ubayy 102
'Abdullah ibn 'Umar 24, 110
'Abdur-Rahman ibn Samurah 101
Abraham 25, 27, 61, 122
Abu Bakr 50, 102, 103
Abu Dharr al-Ghifari 104
Abu Huraira 26, 27, 163, 164
Abu Salama ibn Abd al-Asad 102
Abu Sufyan ibn al-Harith 52
Abu Sufyan ibn Harb 52, 67, 81, 93, 120, 127
Abu 'Ubaydah ibn al-Jarrah 90, 118
Ahadith 74
Al-Harith ibn Suwayd al-Samit 114
Al-Hubab ibn Al-Mundhir 110
'Ali ibn Abi Talib 48, 88, 103, 106, 118, 110
Al-Mujadhdhar al-Dhiyad al-Balawi 114
Al-Waqidi, Muhammad ibn 'Umar 20, 41, 44, 49, 58, 89, 92, 108, 112
Aman: see diplomatic immunity 119
'Amr ibn al-'As 37, 89, 105
Anas ibn Malik 56, 77, 112

Ansar 41, 62, 72, 77, 81, 82, 83, 106
Aristotle 76, 100
'Attab ibn Asid 103
Badr, Battle of 41, 42, 44, 48, 49, 52, 58, 97, 110, 133
Banu al-Harith ibn Ka'b 129, 130
Banu Aws 144
Banu Bakr 124, 127
Banu Jadhima 106, 107
Banu Khazraj 114
Banu Khuza'a 124, 127
Banu Layth 105
Banu Lihyan 93, 94
Banu al-Mulawwah 105
Banu al-Mustaliq 69
Banu Nadir 59, 67, 69
Banu Qurayza 110
Banu Sulaym 105, 113
Banu Thaqif 103
Bashir ibn Sa'd 103, 108
Bay'a 34, 35, 36, 37, 40, 41, 116, 126, 128, 129
Booty: see spoils of war 38, 82, 85, 91, 120
Bible 71
Camel racing 54, 55
Christianity 102
Constitution of Medina 62
Delegation 57, 99, 104, 118, 121, 130
Diplomacy 45, 49, 68, 69, 115, 116,

177

117, 118, 119, 127, 128
Diplomatic immunity 119
Ethos 76
Fadak 69, 127
Friday sermon 74
Ghatafan 67, 68, 69, 94
Hatib ibn Abu Balta'a 112
Hijra 41
Horse racing 54, 55
Hudaybiyyah, Treaty of 34, 37, 45, 46, 62, 68, 69, 112, 117, 119, 122, 124, 126, 127
Hudhayfa ibn al-Yamam 93
Ibn Abi al-'Awja al-Sulami 105
Ibn al-Utbiyyah 113
Ibn Hisham 20, 40, 47, 50, 58, 62, 97, 129
Ibn Sa'd 20, 58, 76, 103, 108
Ijma 109
Ijtihad 108, 109
Ja'far ibn Abi Talib 102
Jesus 17, 18, 19, 25, 31, 32, 63, 72, 109
Jews 43, 62, 63, 64, 68, 69
Juwayriyya bint al-Harith 69
Ka'ba 36, 67, 103, 124, 128
Khalid ibn al-Walid 105, 110, 111, 113, 118, 129
Khalid ibn Sufyan ibn Nubayh al-Hudhali 111
Khaybar 46, 59, 67, 68, 69, 86, 94, 97, 110, 113, 117
Khirash ibn Umayya 106
Khosrow 27
Khums 58, 59
Khutba 73
Logos 76
Ma'bad ibn Abu Ma'bad al-Khuza'i 93
Malik ibn al-Huwayrith 100
Marx, Karl 65

Mecca 26, 28, 35, 36, 37, 41, 42, 44, 45, 46, 52, 61, 63, 64, 67, 68, 69, 70, 74, 78, 80, 81, 83, 86, 92, 93, 94, 100, 102, 103, 106, 111, 112, 113, 118, 119, 120, 121, 122, 123, 124, 125, 126, 127, 128, 129, 131
Medina 36, 41, 44, 45, 47, 48, 57, 59, 62, 63, 64, 66, 67, 68, 69, 80, 81, 82, 83, 86, 89, 92, 93, 102, 112, 113, 116, 118, 121, 127, 132
Military registers 89
Military strategy 65
Morgenthau, Hans J. 175
Mu'adh ibn Jabal 108, 109
Muhajirun 62, 106
Mus'ab ibn 'Umayr 102
Mu'tah 90, 95, 97, 106, 110, 112
Mutilation, prohibition of 74, 90, 91
Nakhla 89
Napoleon Bonaparte 131
Nawfal ibn Mu'awiya al-Dili 42
Nu'aym ibn Mas'ud 93
New Testament 32
Pathos 76
Qur'an 23, 24, 27, 28, 29, 31, 32, 33, 34, 35, 37, 39, 42, 46, 47, 49, 50, 55, 58, 63, 65, 66, 71, 72, 73, 74, 75, 79, 80, 81, 87, 88, 91, 92, 95, 97, 101, 102, 108, 109, 110, 119, 120, 121, 122, 123, 124
Quraysh 44, 45, 46, 53, 67, 68, 70, 80, 92, 93, 94, 95, 105, 110, 123, 124, 125, 127
Qutba ibn 'Amir ibn Hadida 105
Roosevelt, Theodore 87
Ruses 91, 92
Sadaqah 57, 59, 114
Sa'd ibn Abu Waqqas 92
Sa'd ibn Ubadah 82, 102, 113
Safiyya bint Huyayy ibn Akhtab 69

Index

Safwan ibn Umayya 121
Sasanian Empire 27
Sermons 73, 74, 75, 76, 77, 79, 133
Shepherding, leadership as 25,
    26, 109
Shura 39, 44, 45, 132
Spoils of war 46, 82
Strategy 65, 85, 115, 134
Strategic communication 71, 74,
    79, 139
Sunnah 109, 138
Tabuk 48, 49
Ta'if, Battle of 42, 70, 103, 121
Torah, see Bible 32
Tribalism 89, 114, 137
Uhud, Battle of 33, 45, 51, 67, 92, 97,
    100, 103, 106, 107, 110, 114, 133
'Umar ibn al-Khattab 43, 46, 93, 103
Umma 62, 85, 116
'Umra 45, 46, 68
Umm Salama 112
Unity of command 89, 98
Usama ibn Zayd 103
'Utba ibn Rabi'a 80
'Uthman ibn Abu al-'As 103
'Uthman ibn Affan 103
"War is deceit" 92
Zayd ibn Harithah 48, 90, 103
Zakat 57, 64, 66, 108, 110, 118, 129
Zubayr ibn al-Awam 100

Printed in Germany
by Amazon Distribution
GmbH, Leipzig